About the Author

WALTER K. PRICE is pastor of Wood-land Avenue Baptist Church in Lexington, Kentucky, and served as a Southern Baptist evangelist for two years.

Rev. Price was profoundly influenced by the expository writings of H. A. Ironside, he says, and after a careful study of prophecy, Ironside's principles of a premillenial interpretation "provided a satisfactory understanding of what the Holy Spirit was saying."

A graduate of the University of Kentucky and Southern Baptist Seminary, Louisville, Kentucky, Rev. Price entered the pastorate in 1953.

Previous books include *Revival in Romans* and *Channels for Power.*

JESUS' PROPHETIC SERMON

JESUS' PROPHETIC SERMON

The Olivet Key to Israel, the Church, and the Nations

By
WALTER K. PRICE

MOODY PRESS • Chicago

© 1972 by
THE MOODY BIBLE INSTITUTE
OF CHICAGO

Library of Congress Catalog Card Number: 70-175493

ISBN: 0-8024-4330-3

Printed in the United States of America

*Dedicated to my daughters,
Margaret and Sarah*

Contents

Preface

THE KEY to the interpretation of Bible prophecy is to rightly divide the Word of truth concerning Israel, the church, and the Gentile nations. Since this is the key to the prophetic Word in general, it is also the key to Jesus' great prophetic discourse recorded in Matthew 24 and 25. Here He deals with the future and the nation Israel (Mt 24:4-34), the future and the church (Mt 24:35—25:30), and with the future and the Gentile nations (Mt 25:31-46).

As Jesus departs from the temple, both His words and His attitude indicate that this departure is somehow final. This prompts the disciples to ask Him certain questions. In answering their questions concerning when the temple will be destroyed and when the end of the age will occur, Jesus speaks of the future and the Jewish nation that has rejected Him as Messiah, showing that Israel will pass through a time of deepening trouble. The movement of this trouble is indicated by four words that mark the transition from one period to another in Israel's future. These transitions are most clearly noted in the American Standard Version (1901). The tempo of Israel's trouble moves from a time of "travail" to "tribulation" to "great tribulation," followed by a period "after the tribulation" in which Israel will look upon Him whom they have pierced and they shall mourn for Him. Each of these episodes in Israel's future is calculated to ready the nation to accept Jesus as Messiah when He comes a second time.

In addition to Israel's future, because the program of God for the nation Israel does not move in isolation, Jesus deals

also with the future and the church, as well as the future of
the Gentile nations.

The church moves toward its prophetic destiny in what the
apostle Paul calls "the fulness of the Gentiles" (Ro 11:25).
The Gentile nations move toward their climax in the context
of what Jesus calls "the times of the Gentiles" (Lk 21:24).
Each has its place in the great prophetic discourse of Jesus
which He delivered as He sat upon the Mount of Olives
overlooking Jerusalem.

As I reflect upon the content of this book, I would like to
express my indebtedness to two of the greatest Bible teachers
I have ever known. One, Dr. H. A. Ironside, is now with the
Lord. In preseminary days I drank deeply of his words.
I still feel his influence upon my understanding of the pro-
phetic Word.

The other person is of an entirely different eschatological
persuasion. He is Clyde T. Francisco, John R. Sampey Pro-
fessor of Old Testament Interpretation in the Southern
Baptist Seminary. It is he who taught me to keep the message of the Old Testament prophets grounded in relevancy.
I would like to express my appreciation to Dr. Francisco for
many hours of rewarding discussion about the prophets of
Israel. His profound insight into their spiritual message has
been a genuine guide to my premillennialism.

In addition I would like to thank Miss Mary Wood Brown
for help in the translation of some Latin quotations, and
Rabbi William Leffler, of Temple Adath Israel in Lexington,
for discussing with me a number of rabbinic references.
Finally, I express my gratitude to my secretary, Miss Carol
Rawlings, for her gracious work on the manuscript.

Charles H. Spurgeon said of the Revised Version of the
Bible when it appeared in his day that it was "strong in
Greek but weak in English." It is for the former reason that
you will find that the quotations in this book are from the
American Standard Version (1901) of the Bible, which is the

American counterpart of the English Revision of 1881. It is still among the most accurate word-for-word translations of the Bible that we have in English.

1

The Setting of the Sermon

Matthew 23:37-39

TWICE IN THE EARTHLY CAREER of Jesus He climbed a mountain and, having seated Himself, preached to His disciples.

The first of these sermons was preached on a mountain somewhere in Galilee. The exact spot is unknown. This occurred early in Jesus' ministry. The other sermon was preached toward the end of His earthly ministry. The first sermon is known as the Sermon on the Mount. The second is the great prophetic discourse of Jesus, preached on the Mount of Olives just outside the city of Jerusalem. It was preached shortly before His death and is recorded in Matthew 24–25. While it is the Sermon on the Mount that introduces His disciples to a present way of life, it is the sermon on the Mount of Olives that introduces His disciples to the future prospects of Israel, the church, and the nations.

As Jesus nears the end of His earthly life, He takes up those matters that must be dealt with before His time is gone. The issue is this: now that God's people have rejected His offer of the kingdom, what is to be Israel's national destiny? Are all the glorious promises made to her by the Lord through His servants, the prophets, to find fulfillment in some *spiritual* way among all people, rather than in a *literal* way among the nation Israel herself? Will the Jews as a nation ever accept the Lord Jesus Christ as their Messiah? These are the unspoken questions that provide the setting for Jesus' prophetic sermon on the Mount of Olives. Israel had rejected

13

her King; that rejection was soon to be finalized by the cross. Now Jesus must clarify the future of the nation Israel in the light of this rejection. He must also show the relationship between the future of Israel and the church, along with Israel's future and that of the Gentile nations. This must be made clear before His disciples are instructed to carry the gospel to individuals in the Gentile world.

Just before going out on the Mount of Olives, Jesus had pronounced a sevenfold series of woes upon the scribes and the Pharisees (Mt 23:13-36—there are eight woes instead of seven in the King James translation; however, v. 14 is omitted by the R.V. and is evidently a gloss from Mk 12:40 and Lk 20:47). Because the scribes and the Pharisees are the spiritual leaders of Israel, what He says to them is an indictment of the entire nation and her spiritual blindness. Following this indictment of Israel's blind leaders, there is a lament over the city of Jerusalem, (Mt 23:37-39), in which Jesus speaks to the past, the present, and to the future of the spiritually blind nation.

Jesus indicates that there is evidence of this blindness as one examines Israel's *past* history, for the leaders in Jerusalem have always treated the prophets just as they are now to treat Him. They killed the prophets; they will kill Jesus also. "O Jerusalem, Jerusalem, that killeth the prophets, and stoneth them that are sent unto her! How often would I have gathered thy children together, even as a hen gathereth her chickens under her wings, and ye would not!" (Mt 23:37). Every previous attempt of the Lord to bring Israel into a real and meaningful kingdom relationship with Himself has been met with hostility and rejection. It was so in the days of the prophets. It is also true in the day of Jesus, the greatest Prophet. It was true in the days of Zachariah, who was stoned for accusing Israel of breaking the commandments of God (2 Ch 24:20-21). But this blind rejection of the spiritual kingdom which God has intended for Israel was also in evidence in Jesus' day. Interestingly, in pronouncing the series of woes upon the Pharisees, Jesus told them *they* were guilty of the death of Zachariah, though this stoning occurred over eight hundred years earlier: ". . . the blood of Zachariah son of Barachiah, whom *ye* slew between the sanctuary and the altar" (Mt 23:35). Jesus means that the Jews of His day were partakers, with their fathers, in the spiritual blindness that always caused them to reject God's call to deeper kingdom experience. "I would" but "ye would not" (Mt 23:37) has been the debilitating theme of Israel's relationship with God all through the past centuries.

The *present* result of this spiritual blindness, Jesus said, is that "your house is left unto you desolate" (Mt 23:38). If Jesus had Amos 9:11 in mind, then "house" refers to the kingly line of David. Jesus had offered Himself to Israel as David's greater Son and Heir to the throne. He is rejected as Messiah-King and His reign as King in Israel, at least for now, must be postponed. If "house" does not refer to the house of David, then it is a reference to the temple whose destruction is dealt with in the coming prophetic discourse.

However, this condition of spiritual blindness will not be permanent in Israel. A time is coming in the *future* when the nation will say, "Blessed is he that cometh in the name of the Lord" (Mt 23:39). "He that cometh" is a recognized Messianic term. The nation will not always be blind to her Messiah. Israel rejected Him in His first coming. As a result of this rejection "a hardening in part hath befallen Israel, until the fulness of the Gentiles be come in" (Ro 11:25). But in His second coming "there shall come out of Zion the Deliverer; He shall turn away ungodliness from Jacob" (v. 26*b*). It is for this reason that Paul says, "And so all Israel shall be saved" (v. 26*a*). This does not mean that every Jew who ever lived will be saved. Today God deals with the Jew just as He deals with the Gentile; therefore, today any Jew who does not accept Jesus Christ as personal Saviour is lost, just as is the Gentile who rejects Him. But it does mean that the generation of Jews living when Jesus comes again, those who have survived the tribulation, will look upon Him whom they have pierced (Zec 12:10) and be saved.

THE FIRST INTERIM MYSTERY: ISRAEL SET ASIDE IN UNBELIEF

If Israel's house became desolate as a result of the national rejection of Jesus as Messiah when He came the first time, and if the time that Israel will accept Him, saying, "Blessed is he that cometh in the name of the Lord," is at His second coming; what about that time between Christ's two advents? What will happen to the nation Israel during that interim period—already of two thousand years' duration?

The prophetic Scriptures teach two things about Israel in this time between the two advents of Christ which we will call *the interim*. First, it teaches that Israel will not lose her national *identity* during the interim. History has borne out this fact. Nor will Israel lose her national *destiny* during the interim, for her national destiny is inseparably bound up with the covenants that God has made with the nation.

These two things, namely, the fact that Israel has a national *identity* and that she has a national *destiny*, give the ancient people of God a unique place in history. In fact, perhaps the very suffering and persecution which Israel has endured, has held the Jew unique as a national entity. Instead of destroying him, persecution has compressed the Jew into a national unity that is inviolate—even while being disbursed among other nations. Though the lot of the Jew has always been bitter in his exile, in modern times this persecution has intensified. And it may be this very intensification of suffering on the part of the Jew that has caused his smoldering desire for restoration to the ancient homeland to burst into the flaming ambition to regain sovereign control in Palestine. Ezekiel spoke of an earthquake that was to precede the revival of the dry bones (37:7). If the dry bones are the whole house of Israel (37:11) which is restored to the land (37:12), then the earthquake that shook them together in the first place (37:7) might very well be the persecutions which have intensified during the last century. As a result of these persecutions Israel is back in the land today. Ezekiel even pictures present-day Israel having been returned to the land, "but there was no breath in them" (v. 8). There is no breath (*ruach*) or Spirit in them because they are there in unbelief. Therefore, the balance of Ezekiel's prophecy about the valley of dry bones awaits fulfillment at the second coming of Christ when He will breathe spiritual life into Israel.

Late in the nineteenth century, modern anti-Semitism rose in Germany. Soon it spread to Russia and around the world. But this new wave of nineteenth-century persecution became the impetus for returning Israel back to the land within less than one hundred years.

Though Israel has suffered under a series of conquerors from the time of the Assyrian invasion when the Northern Kingdom fell in 721 B.C., through them all she has always managed to maintain a national identity. After the exile the nation returned to her homeland and under the successive overlords of Persia, Greece, and finally Rome she managed to keep a national unity. For a time, after the Maccabean revolt (*c*. 165 B.C.), Israel even knew a short-lived independence. But as the first century A.D. drew to a close a series of events were to bathe the nation in blood and finally dispel her from the land until our day.

The actual revolution which led to this final disbursement of Israel broke out in the procuratorship of Florus in A.D. 66. Florus had attempted to plunder the temple of some of its treasures, an insult which finally aggravated the Jews into a bloody revolt against Rome. Vespasian, one of the greatest of Roman generals, was sent to Palestine to put down the revolt. Soon he was before the gates of Jerusalem. But suddenly Nero died and Vespasian was recalled to Rome and placed on the imperial throne. Vespasian's son, Titus, took command of the Roman forces in Palestine. After five months of horrible suffering, Jerusalem fell in A.D. 70.

Two other vain attempts were made by the Jews in later years to regain their liberties. One was outside Palestine in A.D. 115-17. The other was confined to Palestine. This was the final struggle that Israel as a nation was to make against her enemies until the Israeli-Arab conflicts which arose in the twentieth century.

Israel's final revolt against Rome came during the reign of Hadrian in A.D. 132-35. A Jewish fanatic named Bar Kochba adopted the role of Messiah and led a revolt, probably because Hadrian was about to build a pagan shrine on the temple site. When the Romans put down this rebellion they practically annihilated the Jews. According to a Roman chronicler, 580,000 men were slain and almost a thousand villages were razed. Jerusalem, already in ruins, was completely destroyed. Judea became a desert, depopulated and defoliated. Even the birds avoided it because there was nothing for them to eat. The name of the province of Judea was changed by the Romans to *Palestina,* after the Philistines. Those who were left fled from the land and became scattered among the nations, there to dwell without a home for two thousand years. This is in fulfillment of Hosea 3:4-5, "For the children of Israel shall abide many days without king, and without prince, and without sacrifice, and without pillar, and without ephod or teraphim: afterward shall the children of Israel return, and seek Jehovah their God, and David their king, and shall come in with fear unto Jehovah and to his goodness in the latter days." Though verse 5 will not be fulfilled completely until Christ's second coming, the regathering of Israel, even in unbelief, sets the stage for Israel to actually seek Yahweh their God and David their King.

In 1948 the new State of Israel came into existence in Palestine. This would never have been possible if the Jew had not remained aloof from all the nations in which he dwelt for these many years. The Bible teaches that his refusal to be assimilated among the nations is due to the providential care of God: "And yet for all that, when they are in the land of their enemies, I will not reject them, neither will I abhor them, to destroy them utterly, and to break my covenant with them; for I am Jehovah their God; but I will for their sakes remember the covenant of their ancestors, whom I brought forth out of the land of Egypt in the sight of the nations, that I might be their God: I am Jehovah" (Lev 26:44-45). Today the Jew is what he was centuries ago, both in language, religion, and in national identity. He is back in the land, awaiting the next great event in Israel's history—the time of Jacob's trouble which will purge Israel and ready the nation to accept Jesus as Messiah when He comes again.

The second thing that the prophetic Scriptures teach is that Israel not only has a national identity but she also has a national *destiny*. This means that though the nation has been set aside during the interim, that time between the first and second coming of Christ, God is not yet through with Israel nationally. The fact that God yet has a national destiny for Israel is called a "mystery" by Paul in Romans 11:25. A mystery is something not known in the Old Testament but which is now revealed in the New Testament. Several such mysteries must be understood before one can rightly divide the Word of truth. Next we will look at the church as a mystery. But for now, God's dealing with Israel is called a "mystery" because the time of Israel's setting aside was not known to the Old Testament writers. Paul received this unique revelation concerning Israel's "hardening in part," and brings it out in Romans 11.

The mystery is this: In the interim between the first and

the second coming of Christ the nation Israel will be under God's providential protection but not under His spiritual leadership, for they will not be born again. During the interim, individual Jews may repent and believe and be saved, just as individual Gentiles are saved. But nationally, Israel will lay dormant until they will begin to return to the land in unbelief toward the end of this period. We are witnessing this today. This will ready the stage of history so that once again God can deal with Israel nationally.

What is the basis of this national destiny that guarantees that Israel still has a place in God's plan in spite of her being set aside during the interim? It is the fact that long ago God made certain unconditional covenants with the nation Israel which have never been canceled. They are as valid today as they were in ancient times, for they were not based on the faithfulness of Israel, but on God's faithfulness.

The basic covenant made between God and the nation Israel is recorded in Genesis 12:2-3. The *unconditional* nature of this great covenant made with the nation through Abraham is seen in contrasting it with a later covenant made with Israel at Sinai, the terms of which are clearly *conditional*. In the Sinai covenant the formula, "*If* you will, *then* I will!" is the apparent basis of the relationship between God and Israel as far as temporal blessings and punishment are concerned. But Israel failed to keep the terms of this conditional covenant, expressed in the commandments of God given at Sinai. As a result, the cycle, so prominent in the book of Judges, was set in motion. That cycle of sin, failure, oppression, repentance, restoration, and failure again, was repeated over and over again in the history of ancient Israel.

Finally the exile came. It was then that Jeremiah promised a new covenant (Jer 31:31-34). It was promised because the Sinai covenant was *conditional* and its blessings were contingent upon Israel's faithfulness. Israel needed a new and *unconditional* covenant in which God would do for the nation what they were unable, under the Sinai covenant, to do for themselves. Under the new covenant, God will give them both a new desire and a new power to keep His commandments.

However, there was a covenant made with Abraham centuries before Sinai (Gen 12:2-3). Where Sinai's blessings were conditionally promised, depending upon whether Israel kept the law or not; the blessings of the Abrahamic covenant are *unconditional*. Their fulfillment was not contingent upon Israel's faithfulness. In this covenant God promised certain things to Abraham and to his seed which were arbitrary and not dependent upon the faithfulness of that seed in order to find fulfillment. They were marked by grace and not by the legal equation—"*if* you will, *then* I will"—of the Sinai covenant.

This covenant which gave Israel an *unalterable* national destiny was made originally with Abraham. It was to be restated and elaborated upon in the centuries following his death. This future elaboration enlarged the covenant to cover not only the human seed of Abraham but also the land, the king, and Israel's spiritual redemption. These later embellishments, which further define the original covenant, are called the Palestinian covenant, the Davidic covenant, and the New covenant. Therefore, we have four covenants. But they do not really differ from one another because the essence of all four is contained in the original covenant with Abraham. Thus, there is one great covenant with Abraham, and then three subsequent modifications of that basic covenant. These modifications are found in Deuteronomy 30:1-8; 2 Samuel 7:12-17; and Jeremiah 31:31-34.

With no contingencies, such as Israel's faithfulness, God made certain promises to Abraham which concern the nation Israel even today: "I will make of thee a great nation, and I will bless thee, and make thy name great; and be thou a blessing; and I will bless them that bless thee, and him that

curseth thee will I curse: and in thee shall all the families of
the earth be blessed. . . . Unto thy seed will I give this land"
(Gen 12:2-7). The basic ingredients of this covenant are
restated and reconfirmed on several occasions and are recorded in Genesis 13:14-17; 15:1-21; 17:1-14; 22:15-18.

It should be observed that the parts of the Abrahamic covenant that have been fulfilled have been fulfilled literally.
There is no reason to believe that the rest of the covenant
will not also be literally fulfilled, especially since fulfillment
is not dependent upon Israel's faithfulness to God but upon
God's faithfulness to Israel. Since the Abrahamic covenant
is unqualified and since it promised to Israel a national identity *forever*, these promises *cannot* find subsequent fulfillment in the church.

In Deuteronomy 30:1-8, the part of the Abrahamic covenant related to Israel's possession of the land is restated.
However, this time it is in the context of a Messianic recla-
mation of Israel from the nations among whom God has
scattered her. For the nation is not only brought back to
possess the land promised to Abraham, but when she is
brought back, Israel will be reclaimed spiritually as well as
actually: "And Jehovah thy God will bring thee into the land
which thy fathers possessed, and thou shalt possess it; and
he will do thee good, and multiply thee above thy fathers.
And Jehovah thy God will circumcise thy heart, and the
heart of thy seed, to love Jehovah thy God with all thy heart,
and with all thy soul, that thou mayest live" (Deu 30:5-6).
This can only find fulfillment when the Lord deals again with
Israel at Christ's second coming.

It has been suggested that Deuteronomy 30:9-10 is an ap-
pendix to the covenant that reduces it to a conditional status:
"And Jehovah thy God will make thee plenteous in all the
work of thy hand, in the fruit of thy body, and in the fruit of
thy cattle, and in the fruit of thy ground, for good: for Jehovah will again rejoice over thee for good, as he rejoiced

over thy fathers; *if thou shalt obey* the voice of Jehovah thy God, to keep his commandments and his statutes which are written in this book of the law; *if thou turn* unto Jehovah thy God with all thy heart, and with all thy soul."

However, where verses 1-8 speak to the future of Israel, in verses 9-10, Moses returns to the present and speaks to his contemporaries. After all, Israel's scattering was not an inevitable necessity. They could have retained their national blessings in the land *if* they had obeyed the conditions of the Sinai covenant. But they did not. And therefore the covenant's *conditional* nature permitted Israel's punishment while the *unconditional* promises of the Abrahamic covenant guaranteed final restoration. This passage, therefore, shows how the *unconditional* promises of the Abrahamic covenant and the *conditional* promises of the Sinai covenant can both obtain in Israel.

Not only does the Abrahamic covenant have to do with the nation and the land, but God also said to Abraham, "Kings shall come out of thee" (Gen 17:6). These kings are those who ruled in Judah before the exile. But 2 Samuel 7:12-17 indicates that the royal house of David will possess the throne forever: "And thy house and thy kingdom shall be made sure for ever before thee: thy throne shall be established forever" (v. 16).

To be sure, Jeremiah predicted that the descendants of Jehoiachin, of the house of David, would not continue upon the throne of Judah (Jer 22:30). And they did not, for Jehoiachin was carried captive into Babylon after a short three-month reign (Eze 1:1-2; 2 Ki 24:15) around 597 B.C. Though he was set free thirty-seven years later by Evilmerodach, he never returned to Judah's throne.

Ezekiel carries the pronouncement further, stating that there would never again be a human king of David's line upon the throne of Israel. In chapter 34, he uses the figure of the shepherds of Israel to speak of the former kings of

Israel who have exploited the flock, saying the time has come when God will "cause them to cease from feeding the sheep" (34:10). After the exile no king of David's line ruled upon the throne. Jewish kings ruled in Israel in postexilic days, but they were of another house, descendants in the Hasmonean line (140–63 B.C.).

When given an opportunity to select a ruler, the people did not turn to a living descendant of the house of David, but to Simon, a priest, and elected him as "leader and high priest, forever, until there should arise a faithful prophet" (1 Macc 14:41 f.). Though Josephus says that Aristobulus was the first in the dynasty of the Maccabees to take the title "king,"[1] John Hyrcanus, son of Simon and father of Aristobulus, may have also used the title. These were Jews, but of another line.

However, the line of David had ceased upon the throne of Israel, never again to reign until the prophecy of Ezekiel 34:23-24 is fulfilled when the Lord Jesus Christ, the greater Son of David, reigns during the kingdom age, after His second coming. For this reason the angel spoke thus to Mary about Jesus: "And the Lord God shall give unto him the throne of his father David: and he shall reign over the house of Jacob for ever; and of his kingdom there shall be no end" (Lk 1:32-33).

The prophet Jeremiah states that this reign of the greater Son of David will be fulfilled during a future time of Israel's restoration: "Behold, the days come, saith Jehovah, that I will raise unto David a righteous Branch, and he shall reign as king and deal wisely, and shall execute justice and righteousness in the land. In his days Judah shall be saved, and Israel shall dwell safely; and this is his name whereby he shall be called: Jehovah our righteousness" (23:5-6).

But when will this happen? Will it find fulfillment in some spiritual way in the church? No. It will be fulfilled, he says,

---

[1]Josephus, *Antiquities*, 13, 11, 1.

when Israel is regathered back into the land: "Therefore, behold, the days come, saith Jehovah, that they shall no more say, As Jehovah liveth, who brought up the children of Israel out of the land of Egypt; but, As Jehovah liveth, who brought up and who led the seed of the house of Israel out of the north country, and from all the countries whither I had driven them. And they shall dwell in their own land" (vv. 7-8). Since this did not happen after the Babylonian exile, we must look for a future regathering in which the Lord Jesus Christ will take His rightful place on the throne of David to rule over Israel as King.

Israel continues in spiritual blindness today. Thus, something must happen to them spiritually that will remove their blindness and cause them to believe. Paul said they will experience this hardness *until* the fullness of the Gentiles be come in; then they will be saved (Ro 11:25-26). What will counteract the hardness and remove the spiritual blindness? According to the covenant God made with Israel (Ro 11:27), a Deliverer will come and turn away ungodliness from Jacob. The New covenant which contains this promise is found in Jeremiah (31:31-34) and Ezekiel (36:26-31). However, it is Paul in Romans 11 who connects the fulfillment of the New covenant with the coming of the Deliverer, that is, with the second coming of Christ.

Ezekiel 16 records the allegory of the foundling child who grows up to be a faithless wife. This is a picture of Israel and her numerous infidelities as she perverted God's gifts and blessings. With this awful picture of whoredom one would expect that the Lord is done forever with this faithless people. But just as the prophet Hosea received his faithless wife back and then declared that the Lord would receive Israel back after many years of abiding without a king (3:1-5), so Ezekiel declares that God will remember His covenant with Israel (16:60-63).

Two thousand years already have passed since Israel

nailed her Messiah to the cross. Though individual Jews have
received Jesus as personal Saviour, the nation still abides in
unbelief. But not forever: "In that day will I raise up the
tabernacle of David that is fallen, and close up the breaches
thereof; and I will raise up its ruins, and I will build it as in
the days of old" (Amos 9:11). Perhaps with this passage in
mind, Jesus declared that though the house of David is left
desolate, it will not be forever. For one day Israel shall say,
"Blessed is he that cometh in the name of the Lord" (Mt 23:
39).

In the meantime, no matter how long the interim between
Christ's first and second coming, Israel will have her national
identity preserved, and her national destiny will move unalterably toward the fulfillment promised and so clearly de-
tailed in Scripture. The covenant declared that Israel will
have a land, a King, and a spiritual heritage. God will yet
fulfill His ancient promise to Israel.

THE SECOND INTERIM MYSTERY: THE CHURCH, THE BODY OF CHRIST

James, a half brother of Jesus, quotes Amos 9:11-15 in the
great Jerusalem controversy recorded in Acts 15. He says
the house of David will not be rebuilt until "first God [has]
visited the Gentiles, to take out of them a people for his
name" (15:14). Then, *after these things* I will return, and
I will build again the tabernacle of David, which is fallen"
(v. 16). Only after God has called out a people for His name
from among the Gentiles will David's tabernacle be rebuilt.
This calling out of a people from among the Gentiles occurs
during the interim between Christ's advents. Only after that
time has passed—however long it might be—will the Lord return and again establish David's royal line upon the throne
of Israel.

This brings us to the second thing that must happen in
the interim between Christ's first and the second coming. Not

only will Israel abide in unbelief during this interim—though retaining her national identity and destiny, which is the first mystery—but also during this time the church, the body of Christ, will come into existence. This, too, Paul calls a "mystery" (Ro 16:25).

The word *mystery* appears twenty-seven times in the New Testament. The body of truth referred to as a mystery is that truth which is related in a particular way to this present age. Generally, this present age in which God's mysteries are being fulfilled is the time between Christ's first and second coming. Specifically, it is the time bounded on the one hand by Pentecost, when the church was formed, and on the other hand by the rapture, when the church will be caught out of the earth to meet the Lord in the air.

The several mysteries of the New Testament are revealed to His disciples, for Jesus said, "Unto you it is given to know the mysteries of the kingdom of heaven, but to them it is not given" (Mt 13:11). The seven parables of the kingdom in Matthew 13 seem to be a picture of spiritual conditions that will obtain during the mystery course of this present age.

Though we are concerned here with only two of the mysteries, several others are mentioned in the New Testament. They are the new mystery relationship between Christ and the believer, (Col 1:25–2:3; 4:3), and the development of evil until it reaches its full manifestation in the man of sin (2 Th 2:7); the implications of the incarnation (1 Ti 3:16); the resurrection of the dead saints and the translation of the living saints apart from a general resurrection (1 Co 15:51-52). These are in addition to the mystery of Israel's spiritual blindness during the interim (Ro 11:25); and the mystery of the church as the body of Christ (Eph 1:9; 3:3-9; Ro 16:25).

Because the church is a mystery, this means that it is unknown in the Old Testament. Paul states it this way: "How that by revelation was made known unto me the mystery, as

I wrote before in few words whereby, when ye read, ye can perceive my understanding in the mystery of Christ; which in other generations *was not made known* unto the sons of men, as *it hath now been revealed* unto his holy apostles and prophets in the Spirit; to wit, that the Gentiles are fellow-heirs, and fellow-members of the body" (Eph 3:3-6; cf. Col 1:26). This "body" of which Paul speaks is the church (Eph 1:22-23), a special entity that did not exist until it was created by the Spirit of God at Pentecost.

This means that in the Old Testament the church is nowhere in view. For this reason the Old Testament prophets spoke of things that would occur at Christ's first coming and things that would not occur until His second coming, as one event. They did not see the intervening period—from Pentecost to the rapture—in which God is calling out a people from among the Gentiles to constitute the church, the body of Christ.

This period, already of two thousand years' duration, has been called "The Great Parenthesis" by Dr. Ironside. It is like looking at two mountains in the distance. A valley of great width may separate them, but from a distance it is not seen and the two mountains appear as one mass. The Old Testament prophets saw the events surrounding Christ—some fulfilled in His first coming, some to be fulfilled in His second coming—as one event. This is clear in Isaiah 9:6-7: "For unto us a child is born, unto us a son is given; and the government shall be upon his shoulder: and his name shall be called Wonderful, Counsellor, Mighty God, Everlasting Father, Prince of Peace. Of the increase of his government and of peace there shall be no end, upon the throne of David, and upon his kingdom, to establish it, and to uphold it with justice and with righteousness from henceforth even for ever." The birth of the "child" and the giving of a "son" have obvious reference to Christ's first coming. But the rest of that passage will not be fulfilled until He comes again. But Isaiah spoke of all these events as one because he did not see the great parenthesis—the age of the church—which would separate the two.

Note also that Luke 1:31 was fulfilled in Christ's first coming, but verse 32 will not be fulfilled until His second coming. Jesus recognized this principle, for when He read from the scroll of Isaiah in the synagogue in Nazareth, He stopped in the middle of a sentence. After having read "to proclaim the acceptable year of the Lord," He quit reading, or "he closed the book" (Lk 4:16-20). But in the Isaiah passage (61:1-2) the statement concludes with these words: "and the day of vengeance of our God." Why didn't Jesus read the rest of that statement? Because He read just what pertained to His first coming. The remainder refers to His second coming. Though Isaiah did not see the difference and thus spoke of it as one event, Jesus did.

Paul said this mystery of the church was made known unto him by revelation (Eph 3:3). The Old Testament writer saw the two advents of Christ. But the apostle Paul had the unique distinction of being the first to see that between these two advents Israel would be partially blinded and set aside, and that God would create a new body, the church.

The church came into existence on the day of Pentecost. It was created by that work of the Holy Spirit called the baptism of the Spirit: "For in one Spirit were we all baptized into one body, whether Jew or Greeks, whether bond or free; and were all made to drink of one Spirit" (1 Co 12:13). Each believer on the day of Pentecost was baptized by the Spirit into the body of Christ, the church. All were made one in Christ Jesus.

But this work did not begin and end at Pentecost; it is repeated in each new generation when a person repents and receives Jesus as personal Saviour. At the point of saving faith the new believer is baptized by the Spirit into the body. Therefore, the work of creating the church is still going on, and the church is composed of every born-again believer from the day of Pentecost until this day. This process will continue during this age of grace until the last of the elect is saved. When the last person in the plan of God has been added to the body of Christ by repentance and personal faith in Jesus, the rapture will occur and the church will be caught up to meet the returning Lord in the air.

When the church is removed from the earth, along with the Holy Spirit who created the church and indwells it (2 Th 2:7), then the Lord will again take up His program for the nation Israel. During this following era, known as the tribulation period, God will deal with Israel in judgment and thus ready her to accept Jesus as Messiah and King when He comes to earth the second time at the close of the tribulation period.

Daniel 9:24-27 contains one of the most important and fascinating prophecies in the Old Testament. Considered by many to be the key to understanding God's future program for Israel, it is therefore foundational in Bible prophecy. However, only when the church's mystery nature is understood, along with the fact that the Old Testament writers did not take the age of the church into account when speaking of the Lord's program for Israel, does Daniel's great prophecy of seventy weeks make sense. With the great parenthesis clearly in mind, Daniel's prophecy becomes a key to understanding God's plan for His covenant people, Israel.

Daniel's prophecy is also important because of the chronology it establishes. In it a major outline is given for events from Daniel to Christ, and from the rapture of the church until His second coming. No other passage in the Old Testament does so much to clarify the order of events, as far as Israel is concerned, as does Daniel 9:24-27. In addition, it reconfirms prophecy as that which is to be literally fulfilled. Either Daniel's prophecy must be interpreted literally, or the date of Daniel must be drastically revised—as the critics do.

It is utterly unthinkable to modern biblical criticism that Daniel could have so accurately predicted the future as he does in this and other passages. Therefore, they place his prophecy after many of the events had already occurred in history, and assume that Daniel only treats past history in predictive terms. However, once we accept the fact that this is prophecy—history written in advance—and that the first sixty-nine weeks of the prophecy have already been literally fulfilled, along with some other events which occurred in connection with the fall of Jerusalem in A.D. 70; then it is not difficult to accept the fact that the events of the seventieth week will also be literally fulfilled.

Daniel had been meditating on the years of Israel's exile in Babylon (9:1-2). He understood from the scroll of Jeremiah (25:11-12; 29:10) that the exile was to last for seventy years. The duration of the exile is derived from the fact that Israel had failed to keep the sabbatical year, (Lev 26:34 ff.; 2 Ch 36:21). Every seven years, according to the law of God, the land was to rest. But Israel had neglected this provision, apparently not keeping it for many years. If it took seventy years to pay back the time Israel had failed to keep the sabbatical year, then they must have been neglecting to keep it for 490 years. Thus Daniel could look back over 490 years of failure to that point where God's blessings had ceased. But as he meditates upon this, a vision comes to him in which he is told that *it will be another 490 years before Israel can know the blessings of God again!* It is the events of this future 490 years that make up the great seventy-week prophecy of verses 24-27.

"Seventy weeks are decreed upon thy people" (Dan 9:24). The Hebrew word translated "weeks" means "sevens." A week of years was just as familiar to the Jews as a week of days is to us. For the Jew, a sabbatical year came every seven years, just as a Sabbath day came every seven days (Lev 25: 3-4). Therefore, just as a daily Sabbath ended every week of seven days, so a yearly Sabbath terminated every week of seven years.

Thus, "seventy sevens are decreed," meaning seventy periods of sevens, or seventy times seven, which equals 490 years, are decreed upon Israel. This much time is indicated in order to accomplish in Israel the things that Daniel lists in verse 24*b*: "To finish transgression, and to make an end of sins, and to make reconciliation for iniquity, and to bring in everlasting righteousness, and to seal up the vision and prophecy, and to anoint the most holy." The first three of these seem to refer to what was accomplished as a result of Christ's first coming. The second set of three things will not be accomplished until His second coming. Again, the great parenthesis, the age of the church, that separates the two events in time is unnoted by the prophet.

In calculating the time consumed in this period of seventy sevens, or 490 years, it is well to remember that a biblical year is composed of twelve months of thirty days each (cf. Gen 7:11 and 8:4 with 7:24 and 8:3).

This period begins with the "going forth of the commandment to restore and to build Jerusalem" (Dan 9:25). Only one commandment was given to rebuild the walls of Jerusalem. It was issued by Artaxerxes in 445 B.C. (Neh 2:1-8).

In fulfillment of this great prophecy the prophetic time clock began to tick in 445 B.C. when the command to rebuild the walls was issued. The time involved is seven weeks (49 years), sixty-two weeks (434 years), and the last week of seven years' duration, making a total of 490 years. From the decree to rebuild the walls until the Messiah is cut off is sixty-nine weeks, or 483 years.

Actually, from 445 B.C. until Jesus is crucified in A.D. 29 is 474 years and not 483. There are nine years unaccounted for. Though the text of Daniel 9:26 says "*after* the threescore and two weeks shall the anointed one be cut off," which would allow the leeway, the discrepancy could also be accounted for by changes in the calendar. However, even this is unnecessary, for Daniel 9:26 does not demand that the death of the Messiah take place the minute that the 483 years are over. But the event will occur "after" this time. These 483 years account for only sixty-nine of the seventy weeks. But what about the last week of seven years?

God's prophetic time clock—whose subject is Israel—stopped when the Messiah was cut off after the sixty-ninth week. It has not moved since that time, for in the interim Israel has been set aside. During the great parenthesis, which separates the sixty-ninth and seventieth weeks, God is dealing with the church and not with the nation Israel. However, when the church is caught out of the world at the rapture, that prophetic time clock will move again and the last, or seventieth week, will begin its fulfillment during the tribulation period.

Certain events are predicted in Daniel 9:26 which will happen after the Messiah is cut off, and before the seventieth week. These events affect Israel's *secular* history but are not a part of her spiritual destiny, which falls within the confines of the seventy weeks. Those which affect her historically are the coming of the people of the prince (the Roman army) who will destroy the city and the sanctuary. This terrible period will end with flood, war, and with great desolation (9:26). And so it did in A.D. 70.

After the great parenthesis—the church age which separates the sixty-ninth and the seventieth week—is concluded, God's prophetic time clock will begin to tick again for Israel. During that period of seven years' duration, the prince (the Antichrist, not the Messiah prince, as in v. 25) will make a firm covenant with Israel for one week. But in the midst of the week (i.e., after 3½ years), he will break the covenant that he has made with Israel and cause the sacrifices to cease.

This is the signal for the great tribulation to begin. This time of Jacob's trouble, as the prophet Jeremiah calls it (30:7) will cause great suffering to the people of God, but it will also ready them to accept the true Messiah when He returns to earth at the close of the great-tribulation period (Mal 4:5-6; Lk 1:17; Mk 9:12-13; Mt 11:14).

This time of terrible suffering for Israel, during the seventieth week of Daniel's prophecy, is what Jesus describes in His great prophetic discourse which follows in Matthew 24.

Even though Jesus laments over the city of Jerusalem, He knows that in the interim Israel will not lose her uniqueness. Her identity will remain intact. A Jew is as distinctive today as he was two thousand years ago. His preservation in history is one of God's greatest miracles. In addition, during this interim or great parenthesis, a new witness will come into being. The church will be formed, beginning at Pentecost and continuing until the rapture. When this new mystery—the body of Christ—is completed, Jesus will return and call the church out of the world. Then once again God will deal with His covenant people Israel. History will have run full cycle so that God can deal again with Israel where His relationship to them was broken off two thousand years ago. For in that day world conditions will be similar to those that prevailed in the first century. Israel will be back in the land and again under Roman dominion as they were on that day when Jesus issued His lament and left the temple.

2

Two Questions Concerning the Temple and the Time of the End

Matthew 24:1-3

HAVING DECLARED that Israel's house is left unto her desolate, "Jesus went out from the temple" (Mt 24:1). This closed the last day of His public ministry. It also seems to mark the end of Israel's spiritual life, for no more would the Son of God be found in the temple's sacred precincts.

SIGNIFICANCE OF GOING TO MOUNT OF OLIVES

There may be more than coincidence in the fact that Jesus, having left the temple, went out to the Mount of Olives. To be sure, if He were then on His way to Bethany, the road crossed the Mount of Olives, and it was logical for Him to go that way. However, a deeper significance might relate Jesus' actions to that time when the glory of the Lord forsook Solomon's temple. It took the same route! Ezekiel sees this happening in a series of visions recorded in the early part of his book.

Ezekiel was in Babylon when he had these visions. He had been carried there in the first wave of the exile when Nebuchadnezzar took Jerusalem in 597 B.C. At that time the flower of the population of Judah, including many priests—Ezekiel among them, had been removed to Babylon. He began to prophesy five years later in 592 B.C. Many of his early visions pertained to the people of Judah who were still in the land, for the city of Jerusalem remained populated and intact between 597 and 587 B.C., when it finally fell to another invasion of the Babylonians.

Though the average Hebrew never thought of the Lord as being actually confined to the land of Palestine, he did believe that the worship of the Lord was confined to the land. All other lands were polluted and unclean. For those who had accepted the centralization of worship in the temple in Jerusalem, the logical impossibility of worshiping the Lord elsewhere was apparent. But in a series of visions, Ezekiel sees the Lord forsaking the temple and moving toward the east, the direction of Babylon.

Ezekiel first notes the movement of the glory of the Lord in a vision which he beheld in about 591 B.C.: "And the glory of the God of Israel was gone up from the cherub, whereupon it was, to the threshold of the house" (9:3). The Shekinah glory, which spoke of the Lord's presence, dwelt between the figures of the cherubs above the mercy seat on the ark of the covenant. It was kept in the holy of holies in the inner recesses of the temple. In this verse Ezekiel sees this Shekinah glory leaving the holy of holies and lingering at the door of the sanctuary. As the glory of the Lord stood by the threshold of the house, "the house was filled with the cloud, and the court was full of the brightness of Jehovah's glory" (10:4). The inner court of the temple is filled with the brightness of the Shekinah glory, along the path of departure.

Next Ezekiel sees the glory of the Lord departing from the temple itself through the east gate: "And the glory of Jehovah went forth from over the threshold of the house, and stood over the cherubim," that is, over the chariot that was awaiting to transport the glory of the Lord to Babylon (Eze 10:18). The chariot lingers for a moment at the eastern gate of the temple: "And they stood at the door of the east gate of Jehovah's house: and the glory of the God of Israel was over them above" (v. 19). The last glimpse that Ezekiel has of the glory of God is when it rises above the city and goes out to linger upon the Mount of Olives: "And the glory of Jehovah went up from the midst of the city, and stood upon the mountain which is on the east side of the city" (11:23).

Just as the glory of the Lord departed from the temple of Solomon because the sacred place had been profaned (Eze 7:22), so Jesus leaves the temple and goes out to the Mount of Olives, following the same path.

Though Ezekiel saw the glory of the Lord leave the temple for a while, he also saw it return again. When he describes the ideal temple, one of the things that he notes is the returning glory. It comes from the same direction in which it departed: "Afterward he brought me to the gate, even the gate that looketh toward the east. And, behold, the glory of the God of Israel came from the way of the East" (43:1-2). Ezekiel also notes that when the glory of the Lord returns to the temple, it will never leave again (cf. 44:1-3).

Just so, the Lord Jesus Christ has been rejected by Israel. He leaves the temple. But one day He will come again with power and great glory. When He does, His presence will again fill the temple, for the prophetic Scriptures indicate that there will be a temple during His millennial reign which will be an abiding place for His glory (Eze 43:6-7).

As He departs from Herod's temple, Jesus declares to His disciples that the time is coming when "there shall not be left here one stone upon another, that shall not be thrown down" (Mt 24:2). Herod's temple had been under construction for nearly fifty years when Jesus spoke these words. It was never completed, for in A.D. 70, just a few years later, Jesus' prediction was fulfilled when Jerusalem fell to the invasion of Titus. Josephus describes the fire that consumed the temple when the Roman army had finally broken the resistance of the city:

The flames also spread a long way and roared in unison with the groans of those that were slain, and because the hill was high, and the size of the burning pile so great, one would have thought the whole city had been on fire; nor could one imagine anything either greater or more terrible than the noise. . . . But the sufferings were more terrible than this uproar. For one would have thought that the hill itself, on which the temple stood, was seething hot from its base, so full of fire was it on every side. . . . And now the Romans, as the temple was on fire, judging it idle to spare anything in its vicinity, burnt everything, as the remains of the porticoes, and the gates. . . . They also burnt the treasuries, in which was an immense quantity of money, and an immense number of garments, and other precious things; indeed, to say all in a few words, the entire riches of the Jews were heaped up there, for the rich had built themselves storechambers there.[1]

Because there was much gold stored there, that which had not been previously plundered melted in the fire and ran down among the debris of the fire-gutted temple. The Roman soldiers pulled the very stones apart in order to retrieve this melted gold, and thus the words of Jesus were literally fulfilled!

Two Questions Asked

Following the path of the whirling wheels that had transported the glory of the Lord from Solomon's temple, out through the eastern gate, rising above the city to hover over the Mount of Olives, Jesus and His disciples now make their way out to this same spot on the Mount of Olives. Today the name Mount of Olives is applied to a height which is opposite the old temple area and above a slope that moves downward to the Kidron Valley. There is every reason to believe that this perpetuates ancient Hebrew usage and that this is the same Mount of Olives of Jesus' day. Originally, when named,

[1]Josephus, *Wars of the Jews*, 6:5.

the whole hillside must have been covered with olive orchards. Josephus says that it was a Sabbath day's journey from the city, about a ten-minute walk.

From this summit the holy city lay before Jesus' gaze. There the temple courts would be in plain view. As He *sat* there with the city spread out before Him, His disciples come to Him privately and ask, "Tell us, when shall these things be? And what shall be the sign of thy coming, and of the end of the world?" (Mt 24:3).

Notice the position of Jesus: "He sat." The early church had two forms of oral communication: the *kerygma,* which was preaching to the unsaved; and the *didache,* which was teaching, directed to the believer. The first was done in a standing position. "But Peter, standing up with the eleven," preached to the multitude at Pentecost. However, following the Jewish tradition, teaching was done in a seated position. This is why we speak sometimes of the learning posture in terms of "sitting at one's feet." Jesus *sat,* both when He delivered the Sermon on the Mount (Mt 5:1) and here, when He delivered His great prophetic discourse. Thus He is teaching in order to impart facts of prophetic history and not preaching for a moral decision. Therefore, we are not free to use this material for spiritual moralizing until first realizing its primary intent. It is given as a factual interpretation of history, for even prophecy is history written in advance.

The disciples' questions were based on the assumption that, since Jesus predicted the temple's destruction, the end of the world must be near. They could not conceive of the temple being destroyed except in an apocalyptic context, just as Judah in Jeremiah's day could not conceive of Jerusalem falling while the Lord's temple was there. Nothing short of the climax of human history could affect either the city or the temple—so they thought.

And so this assumption prompts the disciples' two questions: First, "When shall these things be?" In other words, when will the destruction of the temple take place? Then, second, "What shall be the sign of thy coming and of the end of the world?" The second question assumes an inseparable relationship between all these events—the destruction of the temple, Christ's coming, and the end of the world.

Jesus' answer *is* based on the disciples' assumption, for He moves from the fall of Jerusalem and the destruction of the temple, to His second coming at the end of the tribulation period. But, in typical Old Testament fashion, the great parenthesis, or the age of the church, is unnoted in this part of His discourse. It properly belongs between verses 8 and 9. However, like the Old Testament prophets, Jesus moves from near events to those that are far away without noting the great parenthesis between, because at this point He is speaking only about Israel's future. Unless we utilize this Old Testament prophetic precedent and principle, the interpretation of the Olivet discourse would be in hopeless confusion. Though (1) the destruction of the temple, and (2) the Lord's coming, and (3) the end of the world are all connected *logically* in Jesus' answer to His disciple's question, *chronologically* the temple's destruction and the remaining events are separated by the great parenthesis, these centuries in which the church is being called out.

These two questions are a unique feature of the Olivet discourse as recorded by Matthew. In the other two synoptics, Jesus is asked but one question by His disciples: "And as he sat on the mount of Olives over against the temple, Peter and James and John and Andrew asked him privately, Tell us, when shall these things be? And what shall be the sign when these things are all about to be accomplished?" (Mk 13:3). Thus, in Mark's account the disciples ask about the destruction of the temple only. The same is true in Luke: "And they asked him, saying, Teacher, when therefore shall these things be? And what shall be the sign when these things are about to come to pass?" (21:7). In both Mark and

Luke the question is about "these things," that is, about the destruction of the temple which He had just mentioned. Only in Matthew is the second question about the coming of the Lord and the end of the world also asked.

This is not to say that the answer of Jesus, recorded in Mark and Luke, does not mention the distant events. But it does mean that much of His answer, recorded in these two gospels, is related to Jerusalem's destruction. Therefore, the key to interpreting the discourse, as given by Mark and Luke, is the fall of Jerusalem in A.D. 70, while the key to interpreting the discourse in Matthew's account is the tribulation period that immediately precedes Christ's second coming.

God's Program for Three Groups

In 1 Corinthians 10:32 Paul speaks of three groups: the Jew, the Gentile, and the church of God. It is imperative in the interpretation of the prophetic Scriptures to recognize that God has a distinctive program for these three groups. What God has designed for *Israel*, and for the *church*, and for the *nations* must never be confused. They are distinctive groups, and for each of these entities God has a definite program, both in history and in prophecy. Nothing but confusion and misunderstanding can occur when, for example, God's program for Israel nationally is misapplied to the church. Since the church, the body of Christ, was unknown in the Old Testament, God's promises to Israel must find their fulfillment in the nation herself. If they have not yet been literally fulfilled, they will be literally fulfilled when God deals again with the nation after the church is taken out of the world at the rapture. This distinction must also be maintained in interpreting Jesus' Olivet discourse. Though the discourse theme is the nation Israel, because the destinies of the church and the Gentile nations are inseparably bound up with Israel's future destiny, all three groups are considered in the prophetic discourse.

God has a program for the nation *Israel* that is not to be confused with His program for the church. This is the major issue between an amillennial eschatology and that of the premillennialist. The former position holds that God's promises made to Israel in the Old Testament are now to find their fulfillment in the church, which is spiritual Israel. In this position there is no future for Israel as a nation in God's program. Since there is no future for Israel nationally, there is to be no anticipation of a millennial reign of Christ upon earth. Hence "amillennial." The word *millennium* is made up of two Latin words and means "a thousand years." The *a* before the word negates the meaning. Thus an "amillennialist" is one who rejects Christ's thousand-year reign upon earth because he refuses to concede a future for Israel nationally. Under this assumption, all the Old Testament kingdom passages are spiritualized and applied to the church, with no literal fulfillment anticipated. The eternal state will immediately follow Christ's second coming and there will be a general judgment of the saved and lost at the end of time.

Whereas the conservative amillennialist interprets the prophetic Scriptures *seriously* but no*t literally,* the premillennialist interprets them both seriously *and* literally. Therefore, we believe that the nation Israel does have a future in God's program. In fact, we must make this vital distinction between Israel, the church, and the Gentile nations if prophecy is to be interpreted literally and yet not be utterly confusing. The issue, therefore, is not just the interpretation of a single passage in the book of Revelation, as some critics of premillennialism have naïvely suggested. The issue is a whole system of biblical theology. When one realizes the distinction between Israel, the church, and the nations, of great concern is the right division of the Word of truth (2 Ti 2:15).

Israel had its beginning nationally when Abram, a Semite, was called of God out of Ur of the Chaldees (Gen 11:27 ff.).

Along with that call came a covenant (Gen 12:2 ff.) in which the Lord promised that the seed of Abram would become as numerous as the sands of the sea, and that they would forever inhabit the land which God would give them. These people were the elect of God. Their mission was to carry His message of love and redemption to the nonelect. Theirs was a unique distinction which Paul defines as that of "adoption, and the glory, and the covenants, and the giving of the law, and the services of God, and the promises" (Ro 9:4). Because these promises were unconditionally given to Israel, all of them that have not yet been fulfilled will be fulfilled in the future. Hence, God's program for the nation Israel extends from the call of Abraham . Though today God's dealing with the nation is dormant, after the great parenthesis He will deal with them again. First, in a time of purging judgment; then, in a time of national regeneration; and finally, in fulfillment of all the kingdom promises made to the nation long ago.

Again, God has a program for the *church* that is not to be confused with His program for the nation Israel. While it is true that unbelieving Jews are not a part of true Israel (Ro 2:28-29; 9:6-8) and it is also true that only believing Jews are the spiritual posterity of Abraham (Ro 4:11-16; Gal 3:7; 6:15), and in addition, while it is true that believing Gentiles become the spiritual seed of Abraham (Gal 3:14, 29), it does not follow that the church has replaced Israel in God's covenant promises. Rather than the church becoming Israel, individual Jews become members of the church when they are born again. But that is the only connection between the church and Israel.

The church is the body of Christ, composed of all born-again believers. It is bounded on the one hand by Pentecost when the Holy Spirit came to baptize all believers into the body of Christ and thus to create the church. On the other hand it is bounded by the rapture when the church will be caught up to meet the Lord at His return. Therefore, the church's history and experience prove that she has a definite beginning, a definite ending, and is composed of a definite constituency. Only born-again believers are members of the church. It did not exist upon earth in the Old Testament; it will not exist upon earth after the rapture. Before Pentecost and after the rapture, God's program will be the same. His witness to the world will be through the nation Israel. But in the interim between Pentecost and the rapture, the Lord's witness is through the church, empowered by the Holy Spirit (Ac 1:8; cf. vv. 6-7).

In His great prophetic discourse, Jesus does speak to the church (Mt 24:35–25:30), but only to warn her to be watchful and to occupy until He comes. This is the church's sole occupation, for she is the Lord's only witness in this world during this age when Israel is blinded and dormant.

The third distinctive group that appears in the prophetic Scriptures is the *Gentile nations.* God's program for the nations is accomplished during what Jesus called "the times of the Gentiles" (Lk 21:24). Just as the nation Israel is bounded on the one hand by the call of Abraham and on the other by the end of the millennium, and just as the church is bounded on the one hand by Pentecost and on the other by the rapture, so there is a boundary marked off in God's program for the Gentile nations. The times of the Gentiles are bounded on the one hand by the Babylonian Empire and the fall of Judah in 587 B.C. and on the other by Christ's second coming and the Battle of Armageddon. During this entire time Israel "shall fall by the edge of the sword, and shall be led captive into all the nations: and Jerusalem shall be trodden down of the Gentiles, until the times of the Gentiles be fulfilled" (Lk 21:24).

Though Jerusalem has known momentary freedom from

Gentile dominion during past history and even within the times of the Gentiles—for example, during the Maccabean revolt circa 165 B.C., and during the revolt under Bar Kochba circa A.D. 135, and after the Arab-Israeli war of 1967—that freedom has not lasted, nor will it. Though brief historical moments of freedom have come to Jerusalem, the city is destined to be under Gentile dominion when the tribulation period ends. So, even though the city is in the control of the Jews and thus free from Gentile dominion at this writing, this freedom will not last, according to the prophetic Scriptures. Not until the times of the Gentiles are over will Jerusalem be a free city.

The course of the times of the Gentiles is presented in two visions in Daniel. The prophet indicates that while the times of the Gentiles are running their course, four great empires will come upon the world scene: the Babylonian Empire, the Medo-Persian Empire, the Greek Empire, and the Roman Empire. Though these four world empires passed off the scene of history many centuries ago, Daniel indicates that the fourth, the Roman Empire, will be in existence at Christ's second coming.

Again, being consistent with the Old Testament format which does not see the church age, Daniel spoke of the ancient Roman Empire, and the revived Roman Empire, which will rise again at the end of the age, without seeing the great parenthesis that separates the two. He therefore speaks of the Roman Empire as coming into power immediately after the third empire passes away, and existing until the climax of world history. This gives us the boundary of the times of the Gentiles and the empires that will dominate during those times. These empires are five: four in the ancient world, plus the revived Roman Empire at the end of the age.

Since all the prophetic Scriptures revolve around the three groups, Israel, the church, and the Gentile nations, Jesus ad-

dresses them in His prophetic discourse. The discourse falls
into three parts:

1. The future and the nation Israel (Mt 24:4-34).
2. The future and the church (Mt 24:35—25:30).
3. The future and the Gentile nations (Mt 25:31-46).

3

The Time of Israel's Travail

Matthew 24:4-8

THE ANSWERS that Jesus gives to the two questions asked by
His disciples are found in Matthew 24:4-34. The first question, "When shall these things be?" is answered in verses 4-
31. The answer is fourfold. "These things shall be," Jesus
answers, "in the context of a time of progressive difficulty for
Israel." The time sequence and the progressively deepening
difficulty for Israel can best be noted by the four words that
are used to mark the transition in Jesus' discourse. These
four words stand out most clearly in the American Standard
Version, for it translates them all differently, where the King
James Version and other versions do not. The four words are
"travail" (v. 8), "tribulation" (v. 9), "great tribulation" (v.
21), and "after the tribulation" (v. 29). In themselves, apart
from the elaboration that Jesus gives them, these words suggest two things: First, they set forth a *time sequence*. Second, they suggest an *intensity sequence*. Thus, from both a
quantitative and qualitative standpoint, Israel is due for a
time of increasing difficulty.

Granted that both the *time* and *intensity* sequences are
here, to what period in Israel's history do they refer? It is
rather obvious that the last three, "tribulation," "great tribulation," and "after the tribulation," refer to that time in the
future when the Lord will deal with Israel again, as set forth
in Daniel's seventieth week. If this premise is granted, then

the time of Israel's *travail* must be located somewhere in history between the time that Jesus spoke these words and the time of the tribulation period. That is, the time of Israel's *travail* must fall somewhere in the great parenthesis—between the cross and the rapture.

The time of Israel's *travail*, set forth in verses 4-8, *could* cover that time in Israel's history during the last two thousand years when the Jews are scattered among the nations. During this period the Jews have known travail. They have suffered—not as severely as they will suffer during the tribulation—but the wandering Jew has been marked by travail rather than tranquillity.

However, the key to the exact location of this time period, which Jesus calls the *travail* of Israel, may be found in Daniel's prophecy of the seventy weeks (9:24-27). Daniel sees two periods of Israel's suffering *after* the anointed One is cut off, that is, after the death of Jesus, Israel's Messiah, upon the cross. First, Daniel sees clearly the time of the end when the Antichrist will break the covenant he has made with Israel during the midst of the week (9:27). This violation of the covenant will usher in great suffering for Israel. This is clearly a great tribulation event.

But Daniel also sees a time, *immediately* after the anointed One is cut off, when there will also be suffering for Israel. It is that time when the people of the prince, the Roman army, will come and destroy the city and the sanctuary. "And the end thereof shall be with a flood, and even unto the end shall be war; desolations are determined" (9:26). The fulfillment of this was climaxed in A.D. 70. Therefore, the time of Israel's travail, given in Matthew 24:4-8, must refer to that same time period which ran its course between the Olivet discourse and the fall of Jerusalem in A.D. 70.

The era between Christ's death and Jerusalem's fall, covered by Matthew 24:4-8, was marked by a time of bitter trouble for the Jews. History, both secular and sacred, confirms this.

Archaelaus, son of Herod the Great, ruled in Judea, Samaria, and Idumea between 4 B.C. and A.D. 6. During his reign Mary and Joseph returned to Israel from Egypt. When the misrule and tyranny of Archaelaus caused both the Jews and Samaritans to request his removal, Augustus banished him to Gaul. With this removal of their ruler by their own request, the Jews in Judea had forfeited the last vestige of political independence. Power passed to the Roman procurators. The Maccabean request for Roman aid had reached its logical consequence. No longer was Judea to be governed by a Jew.

Four Roman procurators ruled in Judea before Pilate, but from the procuratorship of Pilate (A.D. 26-36) to that of Florus (A.D. 64-66), Jewish resentment of Roman rule intensified. During the rule of Florus, the last and apparently the worst of the Roman procurators, the long-checked outbreak of the Jews began. This rebellion was to bring the Jews into confrontation with the full force of the Roman Empire.

The four years prior to A.D. 70, which probably mark the real focal point of the time of *travail* in Matthew 24:4-8, found Palestine in wild fury, for not only were the Jews contending with the Romans, but there was civil war among the Jews themselves. The only parallel in modern history would be the worst days of the French Revolution or the Russian overthrow of Czarism. Though Josephus often exaggerates, his chronical of the horrors of those days is full of precise details of ruthless cruelty. The Jewish Midrash on Lamentations also throws much light upon this era.

It all began when the Roman procurator Florus became irritated by a group of Jews in Caesarea due to their dispute with some Greeks over the right of way for a synagogue. The Jews insulted Florus who, in turn, scourged and crucified a number of Jews. The resulting rebellion soon spread all over

Palestine. When the Syrian legate marched against Jerusalem, he was defeated. This temporary victory caused many otherwise neutral Jews to rally to the cause.

In A.D. 67 the revolt was put down in Galilee, but continued in Judea, while civil conflict erupted in Jerusalem. Three Jewish factions fought within Jerusalem as the city was drawing siege from the Romans without. Incidentally, during this turmoil and while the city was under Roman fire, Rabbi Johanan ben Zakkai escaped from the city and, coming to the Roman general, requested to be allowed to start a school at Jabneh (Jamnia). The request was granted. This seemingly trivial request saved Judaism from extinction.

Finally, amid famine and disease, the city which had been under siege for many months fell. Even when the outer walls of the castle of Antonia and the temple had been breached by the Romans, the Jews were still fighting among themselves in the Upper City. Upon the 10th of Ab in the year A.D. 70, amid circumstances of unparalleled horror, Jerusalem was taken by the Romans. The temple was burned and the Jewish state was no more. The Romans struck a commemorative coin to memorialize Judea's fall. On it was the figure of a woman mourning beneath a palm tree. *Judea Capta*—Judea taken captive—was inscribed thereon.

It was this era of Jewish history that Jesus is describing prophetically in Matthew 24:4-8. One could be reminded of that *travail* even today in some parts of Europe. For there, since the Middle Ages, Jews have been pursued by their tormentors who shouted, "HEP! HEP!" This is a takeoff on the Jewish lament, *Hierosolyma est perdita*—"Jerusalem is lost." This is indeed, for Israel, a time of *travail*, but it is only the beginning of her sorrow (v. 8). The horror-filled days of the late 60s, which led up to the fall of Jerusalem in the year 70, can only be a preview of the much greater horror that is to befall Israel in her latter days.

First Mark of Travail: False Christs

This time of travail between Christ's death and the fall of Jerusalem is marked by three things. First, there will arise false Christs: "For many shall come in my name, saying, I am the Christ; and shall lead many astray" (v. 5). Notice that the rise of false Messiahs will occur during three different periods of Israel's prophetic history. Jesus warns of them in verse 5, but He also returns to this warning in verses 11 and 24. However, He is not repeating Himself. He is saying that false Messiahs will occur during both the time of Israel's travail and also during the tribulation period.

Verse 5 speaks of the false religious leaders that emerge during the time of Israel's travail in those years just before the fall of Jerusalem in A.D. 70. Undoubtedly, it was the rumors of wars and the earthquakes and famines that called forth these wild Messiahs who foretold miracle victories without armed conflict. Three of these first-century false Messiahs are mentioned in the book of Acts: Theudas (5:36), Judas of Galilee (5:37), and "the Egyptian" (21:38). It is unavoidable that false religious leaders would emerge during a time of national conflict.

As the chaos continues toward the end of the decade of the 60s, Messianic fanaticism was inevitable. Josephus tells of the Egyptian who came to Jerusalem, saying that he was a prophet.

> and advised the multitude of the common people to go along with him to the mount of Olives, as it was called, which lay over against the city, and at the distance of five furlongs. He said further that he would shew them from hence, how, at his command, the walls of Jerusalem would fall down; and he promised them that he would procure them an entrance into the city through those walls, when they were fallen down. Now when Felix was informed of these things, he ordered his soldiers to take their weapons, and come against them with a great number of horsemen and footmen,

from Jerusalem, and attacked the Egyptian and the people that were with him. He also slew four hundred of them, and took two hundred alive. But the Egyptian himself escaped.[1]

Josephus also mentions another "imposter" who appeared in those days among the villages of Judea, promising deliverance and freedom to the people if they would follow him.[2]

Again he tells of Theudas who claimed to be a prophet:

[He] persuaded a great number of people to take their effects with them and follow him to the river Jordan; for he told them that he was a prophet, and that he would, by his own command, divide the river, and afford them an easy passage over it, and many were deluded by his words. However, Fadus did not permit them to make any advantage of his wild attempt, but sent a troop of horsemen out against them; who falling upon them unexpectedly, slew many of them, and took many of them alive. They also took Theudas alive, and cut off his head, and carried it to Jerusalem.[3]

These are the false Messiahs that we know by name. Many others must have appeared in that same era. In fact, Josephus says the chief incentive for war against the Romans was this rash of spurious Messiahs who arose between the Lord's ascension and the Jewish war to fan the flames of revolt. It is interesting that no false Messiahs arose to claim that title before the first century. However, during the first century the Jews were given over to the delusions of many deceptive religious leaders. But this is exactly what Jesus predicted would occur during the years of Israel's *travail*.

The last of the false Messiahs to appear within the time of Israel's travail was Bar Kokhbah. Though he appeared over fifty years after the fall of Jerusalem, he is to be noted for it was he who led the Jews in their terminal conflict with Rome

[1]Josephus, *Antiquities*, 20, 8, 6.
[2]Ibid., 20, 8, 10.
[3]Ibid., 20, 5, 1.

in about A.D. 135. Nothing is known of his early life; he appears when open conflict had already broken out with Rome.

Two things seem to have set off this final revolt by the Jews. One was the visit to Jerusalem of the Roman emperor Hadrian, who issued an order while there for the resumption of the rebuilding of the city. This was regarded by the Jews as a final gesture of contempt and subjection and not to be taken without a struggle. A second thing that Hadrian did was to reissue the edict of Domitian prohibiting bodily mutilation. Though not specifically directed toward the Jews, it obviously affected the practice of circumcision.

The Jews were now ready to follow anyone who would lead them in a new revolt against Rome. So when the courageous fighter Bar Kokhbah appeared he naturally took on himself the aura of the long-awaited Messiah. Later tradition has it that he was an only son of the house of David, both of which were Messianic necessities. On one occasion Bar Kokhbah caught a stone which had been shot from a Roman catapult and threw it back. Hearing of this, Rabbi Akiba exclaimed that this man must really be the King Messiah, and gave him the name "Bar Kokhbah," taken from Numbers 24:17:"There shall come forth a star *[kokhab]* out of Jacob."

SECOND MARK OF TRAVAIL: ARMED CONFLICT

Second, the eve of Israel's *travail*, prior to A.D. 70, is to be marked by armed conflict, both actual and threatened: "And ye shall hear of wars and rumors of wars; see that ye be not troubled: for these things must needs come to pass; but the end is not yet. For nation shall rise against nation, and kingdom against kingdom" (Mt 24:6-7*a*). Christ's lifetime was marked by an era of peace. After the death of Augustus Caesar in A.D. 14 the people began to realize that the Pax Romana, "The Roman Peace," was not something one man had produced. It was a time of enforced peace brought on by a system of Roman government. Though conquered races lamented their loss of independence and chafed under the imperial yoke, the Pax Romana was a priceless benefit even to them. Wars had ceased. Civilization was advanced. Commerce flourished. In peaceful rivalry ancient hostilities were forgotten—for a while. However, Jesus saw that this time of enforced tranquillity would not last. Soon all the land would be rift with wars and rumors of wars.

Conflict was of two kinds in Judea: from within and from without. The former was a three-cornered civil conflict brought on by Jewish Zealots fighting with other Jewish Zealots. This internal conflict inevitably brought down the wrath of the Romans.

Between A.D. 44 and 66, while Judea was ruled by no less than seven Roman procurators, the Jews were in a perpetual state of internal stress, rage and frenzy. The Zealots, and later the Sicarii, adopted the most extreme measures in opposing Rome. The latter group was so named because they armed themselves with short daggers (*sicae*) and, mingling among the crowds at festival time, stabbed their enemies to death. They terrorized Jerusalem, and when the city finally fell to the Romans, three groups of Zealots within were fighting against each other.

John of Gischala, a leading Zealot, had established himself in the temple court. While John held the temple hill and the castle of Antonia, another Zealot group, Elazar and his band of Zealots, held the inner temple. At the same time Simon bar Giora, with a third Zealot band, held the Upper City. While the Roman army was reducing the countryside from without, the Zealots were locked in civil conflict within the walls of Jerusalem.

However, the *travail* of Israel was not only from internal and civil strife, but Israel's ultimate destruction issued from without. The great Roman general Flavius Vespasian had been called out of retirement by Nero to command the attacking Roman forces. On his way to Judea, Vespasian picked up the fifth and tenth Roman legions at Antioch in the winter of A.D. 66/67. In the spring of A.D. 67 he joined his son Titus who was bringing the fifteenth legion from Egypt. In addition his army was composed of twenty-three auxiliary cohorts and six squadrons of horses.

Jewish tradition, as reflected in the Midrash on Lamentations (1:31), indicates that there were also four native commanders with their respective armies from Arabia, Africa, Alexandria and Samaria. The total strength of Vespasian's army was estimated to be 60,000. It took the Romans a few years to subdue the rebellious countryside and to free the army to attack the city. Vespasian's first aim was to subdue the wealthy and populous area of Galilee.

The Jewish historian, Josephus, was in the fortress of Jotapata in Galilee when it was captured by the Romans. Though many of the Jews there preferred death to capture, Josephus tells how he escaped the Romans and finally gave himself up to Vespasian.[4] Though the Roman commander intended to send him to Nero to be tried, Josephus delayed his punishment by prophesying that both Vespasian and his son, Titus, would become emperors. When Vespasian heard that other of Josephus' prophecies had come true, he began "to treat him with kindness and solicitude," though, for the time being, he was not released from his chains.

Vespasian systematically reduced the resistance of the Jews in Galilee. The whole region was depopulated: 6,000 youths were sent to Corinth for slave labor, 1,200 old men were killed, and the remaining Jews, more than 30,000, were sold as slaves. In the fall of the fortress of Gamala, 4,000 Jews were massacred, not including those who had taken their own lives rather than surrender to the Romans.

Finally in the fall of A.D. 69 an immense army marched on Jerusalem, one of the best-fortified cities in the world. Pro-

[4]Josephus, *Wars,* 3:430-34.

tected on three sides by deep ravines, on its ridges were high walls also. Only on the north side was the land flat, but here three walls protected the city. Within the city was another high point where the temple was located. This was the best-protected point of all, for the fortress of Antonia blocked any access to it.

The Romans set one legion on the Mount of Olives and another on Mount Scopus, vantage points from which they could survey all that transpired within the city. Assault machines were constructed by cutting down all trees surrounding the city—much of the landscape remained denuded until the reforestation program Israel instituted in this century.

Each successive wall in turn fell to the Romans' siege towers and battering rams. In May the outer wall, or the "third wall," fell; five days later the "second wall" fell. After some temporary delays, two Roman legions finally breached the walls into the Tower of Antonia in July, A.D. 70. From here they reached the streets of the city. The Jews fled to the temple. With the fall of the tower, victory was assured.

Titus called a council together to discuss the fate of the temple. Some thought it should be completely destroyed because it had always been a rallying point for the resistance. Others thought that it should only be destroyed if the Jews fortified it for purposes of warfare.[5] Josephus says that Titus wanted to save it, but others declare that it was Titus himself who made the decision that it should be destroyed.

For a week the Romans battered at the gate. Finally, by setting fire to the gate they gained an entrance. The Jews retreated to the inner court of the temple. When the inner court was taken by the Romans the next day, great numbers of Jews were killed. Those Jews who remained then gathered in the holy place.

On the ninth of Ab, the same day the Babylonians had captured the temple 657 years before, the Romans set fire to the

[5]Ibid., 6:236-40.

temple. Only a part of the western wall—the Wailing Wall of our day—was left standing. According to the Midrash, this was due to the failure of one of Titus' officers who failed to carry out the task of full destruction. His excuse to Titus was that he wanted to leave a monument standing to the Roman victory. But this did not save him; he was killed for failing to carry out to the fullest the orders of Titus.

So accurately were Jesus' words fulfilled in these years that surround the fall of Jerusalem that many liberal critics assume that they could not have been written until after the events had taken place.

THIRD MARK OF TRAVAIL: FAMINES AND EARTHQUAKES

The third mark of Israel's time of *travail* is that of famines and earthquakes in divers places (v. 7*b*).

Twice a famine occurred in Rome during the reign of Claudius (A.D. 41-54). These famines increased as the years passed. Someone has said that "it takes a hungry nation to make a revolution." Judea's economic distresses were widespread and increasing in the days that led up to the final revolt. The government tried to relieve the distress, but with little effect. Hungry men formed themselves into bands called "brigands" to rob the rich and feed the poor. In the end these "brigands" became the *sicarii*, the "men of the knife" who incited the people to rebellion.

Famine is recorded as occurring in Palestine in Acts 11:28 and also during the reign of Claudius. That Rome itself was famine-stricken suggests that Egypt and Africa suffered from famine also, for Rome was dependent upon imports of food from these provinces. Another famine occurred during the reign of Nero (A.D. 54-68). However, the most dramatic description of famine among the Jews comes from the pen of Josephus who pictured the starvation that accompanied the siege of Jerusalem:

> And famine increased its dimensions, and devoured the
> people by whole houses and families; the roofs were full of
> women and children that were dying of starvation, and the
> lanes of the city were full of dead bodies of the aged; the
> children also and the young men wandered about the mar-
> ket-places like shadows, all wasted away with famine, and
> fell down dead, wherever death seized them.[6]

As the famine grew worse the Romans added to the Jews'
suffering by displaying tempting food where it could be seen
from the city.

> Now the number of those that perished by famine in the
> city was prodigious; and the miseries they underwent were
> unspeakable; for if so much as the shadow of any kind of
> food anywhere appeared in any house, a fight ensued, and
> the dearest friends fell to contending with one another for
> it, snatching from each other the wretched supports of life.
> . . . And their hunger was so intolerable, that it obliged
> them to chew anything, and they picked up such things as
> the filthiest animals would not touch, and actually ate them.
> Nor did they at last abstain from girdles and shoes, and
> pulled off and gnawed the very leather which belonged to
> their shields. And wisps of old hay became food to some.[7]

The famine in Jerusalem had been hastened and aggravated by the fact that immense supplies of grain had been
intentionally destroyed by Jews themselves. This grain was
stored in Jerusalem around the temple. However, so fierce
was the hatred between groups of rival Zealots that one group
burned the grain—even though the Roman siege was imminent—rather than see it fall into the hands of other Zealots.
Another story in the Midrash tells how the Sicarii, determined to force the rich citizens to action in the revolt, had
actually fired the warehouses containing the corn stored there
against the siege. It even specifies the names of three of

[6]Ibid., 5, 12, 3.
[7]Ibid., 6, 3, 3.

these rich citizens whose stores were burned: Ben Kalba Shabua—so called because anyone coming to him, hungry as a dog (*kalba*), went away satisfied, says the Talmud (Gittin 56*a*), Ben Zizit ha-Kesset, and Naqdimon ben Gorion. Ancient estimates were that each of these stores could have fed the country for ten years.

Other stories in the Midrash tell how the Jews would at first lower baskets of gold to the Romans who would give them baskets of wheat in turn. They then received baskets of barley in exchange for gold, then straw, and finally nothing (1:39). Many of these sad stories are contained in the Midrash on Lamentations. Outside the walls the Romans would roast goats, the smell of which would drive the starving people delirious (4:12). The aqueduct that had brought water was broken, and water became scarce (4:7). A woman tried to sell her bracelet for food. When she could not, she fell dead (2:16).

When Rabbi Johanan saw men boiling straw and drinking the juice, he realized that the days of Jerusalem were over, for these men could not stand against the legions of Vespasian, and he knew that if the Torah was to survive he had to escape from the city. It was not easy to do, but by a ruse he succeeded, and wandered straight into the Roman camp, where he was arrested (1:31).

Although the famines of the ancient world are rather well documented and thereby enable us to know for certain that they were peculiarly intense during this time before the fall of Jerusalem, the documentation for great seismic activity may not be as extensive. Nevertheless, Josephus in his biography mentions an earthquake that occurred in Jerusalem. We do know that a great earthquake occurred in Crete in A.D. 46 or 47. Another shock was felt in Rome during the reign of Nero in A.D. 51. One was recorded in Phrygia in A.D. 53, and another in Laodicea in A.D. 60.

Seneca wrote in his epistles in about A.D. 64, "How often

have the cities of Asia fallen, how often have those of Achaia fallen at tremor? How many towns of Syria, how many in Macedonia have been devoured? How often has this destruction laid waste Cyprus? How often has it overthrown Paphos? Often there has been reported to us the destruction of entire towns." There may have been a rash of earthquakes about this time that caused the Roman philosopher to write as he did.

Jesus said that these things would occur "in divers places," that is, "here and there." There have always been famines and earthquakes, but Jesus' words would suggest that their frequency would increase in all localities during this time.

All these things are the beginning of *travail*. In latter years the memory of Israel's travail was too bitter to be borne. The Midrash says that Rabbi Gamaliel, awakened in the night by a woman crying, would think of the destruction and weep so much that his eyelashes were washed away (1:24). Rabbi Johanan used to expound a certain verse from Lamentations in sixty ways, but Rabbi Judah Ha-Nasi only in twenty-four, because after that he would break down at the recollection of so much unhappiness (2:4).

But *travail* is a lesser word than *tribulation*. As intense as the suffering was during the closing days of the Jewish state in the A.D. 60s, a time of *tribulation* is yet to come upon the people of Israel. However, this time of *tribulation*, described in Matthew 24:9-14, will not come upon Israel until after the church age has run its course. Therefore, the great parenthesis belongs between verses 8 and 9.

4

The Course of the Church Age

THE AGE OF THE CHURCH separates Matthew 24:8 and 9. However, this era, already of two thousand years' duration, is skipped in typical Old Testament fashion. Jesus is dealing with Israel's national destiny. The church plays no part in that national destiny. Therefore, the thought of Jesus moves from the *travail* that came upon the nation in the first century, to the time of *tribulation* that will come upon the nation in the future, with no mention of the church which is called into being in the interim between these two events.

God's time clock for Israel stopped ticking when the Messiah died upon the cross. The pendulum has not moved since. But one day, when God has finished calling out from among both Jews and Gentiles a people to constitute the church, then the pendulum will move again. When it does, God's program for the nation Israel will begin its final stage of fulfillment.

Paul speaks of this age—between Pentecost when the church is called into being, and the rapture when the church is caught out of the world—as the "fulness of the Gentiles" (Ro 11:12, 25). This is different from the "times of the Gentiles." The "times of the Gentiles" is that period in which the nation Israel in general and the city of Jerusalem in particular will be under the control of one form or another of Gentile power (Lk 21:24). The times of the Gentiles runs its course between the Babylonian exile and the Battle of Armageddon. But the "fulness of the Gentiles" is a term that

61

Paul uses in Romans 11 to refer to that time when the church, the body of Christ, is being created, and especially to that time when its completion is being contemplated.

Paul speaks of the fulness of the Gentiles in connection with Israel, whom he calls the natural olive branches (Ro 11:17 ff.). The nation Israel, these natural branches, has been broken off in order that the wild olive branches might be grafted in. The wild olive branches represent the church composed largely of Gentile believers. It is the process of the engrafted wild branches that will continue until "their fulness" is realized (Ro 11:12). When the church is complete, then the Lord will turn again to deal with the natural olive branches, the nation Israel (vv. 23-24).

The whole point of Paul's argument in Romans 11 is that the nation Israel has been set aside. God has turned to the Gentiles to call out from among them a people to constitute the church. But when this calling out is finished and the church which is the body of Christ is completed, then God will turn again to deal with Israel nationally.

This present age in which the church is called into being runs its course between two clearly defined points. The church began at Pentecost when the Holy Spirit came to baptize all born-again believers into the body of Christ. The Holy Spirit continues to do this work today and will continue to do so until the church, the body of Christ, is complete. When the last of the elect is saved and added to the body of Christ, the church will then be caught away to meet the Lord in the air. This event is called by many "the rapture of the church." The word *rapture* does not appear in Scripture in our English translation. It comes from a Latin word which means "to seize" or "to snatch away," the word that Jerome used in his Latin Vulgate translation of 1 Thessalonians 4:17.

The church age, which is bounded on the one hand by Pentecost and on the other hand by the rapture, is characterized in the seven letters to the churches in Asia, found in

Revelation 2—3. Granted, these letters do have a *historical interpretation.* There is no doubt that there were seven literal and historic churches located in the Roman province of Asia, and what is said to these churches has to do with actual and local needs. These are real first-century churches with actual problems to which the Lord addresses Himself in these letters.

There is also a *spiritual application.* The spiritual principles in these letters are above the local situation and are relevant to every believer in every age.

But in addition there is in this series of letters a *prophetic revelation.* These letters present the condition of the professing church from its beginning in the first century until the end of the church age, with each church addressed representing a successive era in church history. This does not mean that each letter represents a pigeonhole into which the various centuries since the founding of the church can be neatly placed; the issues are not that clearly defined. However, each successive letter does give an impression as to the movement of the church's history, and therefore, they characterize the history of the church in such a way as to let us know that we are not to expect a steady movement from weakness to victory.

Many believe that the church will eventually triumph in the world. But this is not the picture of the church given in the seven letters. Rather, the church moves in cycles. There are times of dearth; there are times of revival. However, the general direction of the spiral is downward instead of upward. The church will come to the close of the age, not in victory but in defeat, for the end of the church age is marked by apostasy instead of triumph.

Ephesus means "desired." The church at Ephesus (Rev 2:1-7) represents the spiritually declining church toward the end of the first century A.D. It is the apostolic church which has left its first love. The first century of faithfulness to the Lord is now over and the zeal of the church begins to fade.

Smyrna represents the persecuted church of the second and third centuries (Rev 2:8-11). The name Smyrna means "myrrh." Like myrrh, whose fragrance is produced by crushing, the church in these days gave off its fragrance through the persecution which it suffered. The city of Smyrna was located about thirty-five miles north of Ephesus. It was a seaport town like Ephesus, but unlike Ephesus, which today is a desolate swamp, Smyrna (the modern Turkish city of Izmir) is a thriving community with a large population.

Here the martyrdom of Polycarp, bishop of Smyrna, took place in the second century. On a festival day, the crowd, excited by the Jews, seized Polycarp and gave him the choice: worship Caesar or die! He replied, "Eighty and six years have I served Christ and He has never done me wrong. How can I blaspheme my King who saved me?" Though it was on a Sabbath day, the Jews helped gather wood for the fire and Polycarp was burned to death. But his experience was that of the whole church in this era. It suffered much persecution and, though many lapsed, others stood strong in the face of persecution.

Only this church and the one in Philadelphia received no word of condemnation in these letters. A tribulation of ten days is determined upon this church—or upon this era (Rev 2:10). Barclay says that this is a general Greek term meaning "a short time." However, there is an interesting fact presented in Fox's *Book of Martyrs*. The first chapter of this classic work, which was written in the sixteenth century, is entitled "Ten Primitive Persecutions." Here he lists ten different persecutions of the church that resulted from ten different edicts of the Roman emperors from Nero to Diocletian (A.D. 54-305). All but two of these occurred in the second and third centuries A.D.

Thus these ten days speak of ten episodes of persecution,

which takes the history of the church down to the time of Constantine. These were years of great suffering for the church, but this was also a time of the church's greatest witness: "I know thy tribulation, and thy poverty (but thou art rich)" (v. 9).

Pergamum (Rev 2:12-17) means "thoroughly married." This letter pictures a time when the church became completely wedded to the world. The day of the church's persecution had passed in history, and in this era it was popular to be identified with the church. This came about through the "conversion" of the Roman emperor, Constantine. Constantine's father had been made ruler of Britain and Gaul by the emperor Diocletian. Upon his death, Constantine became ruler of Gaul, and for a while was content. Then, fired with ambition to rule the empire, he invaded Italy and headed for Rome. When he reached the Tiber River he supposedly had his celebrated vision. In the afternoon sky he saw a bright cross on which were the words, "In this sign conquer." He dreamed that night that Christ bade him take the cross for his standard. The date was October 28, A.D. 312. Defeating Maxentius, Constantine became Caesar of the western half of the empire. In A.D. 313 he issued the famous Edict of Milan which gave Christians the right to practice their faith openly. With this the persecution of the church ceased.

The church of Pergamum is censured for holding the "teaching of Balaam" (2:14). It was Balaam who was forbidden to curse Israel as the king of Moab wanted him to do. Unable to curse Israel for profit, Balaam then suggested to the king how he might defeat Israel, for example, by enticing Israel to intermarry with the Moabites, and thereby encouraging idolatry among them (Num 25:1-5; 31:13-15). Hence the teaching of Balaam was that of intermarriage and spiritual compromise—a perfect picture of the church during the time from Constantine on through the Middle Ages.

The issue is not orthodoxy but compromise. The church remained orthodox during this time. In fact, it was during the reign of Constantine that one of the greatest battles for orthodoxy was won. Arius, a minister in Alexandria, had taught that while Christ was more than human, He was less than God, a creature halfway between God and man. Athanasius took issue with this teaching, declaring that if Christ is halfway between God and man, He is neither God nor man. The controversy became so great that it threatened to divide the church. On July 4, A.D. 325, Constantine called a council of bishops to meet at Nicaea and settle the matter. The emperor himself presided at the council. The matter was settled against Arius and later the Nicene Creed, which reflected this decision, was drawn up. It declared that Jesus is the "only begotten of the Father, very God of very God, begotten, not made, being of one substance with the Father." Arius had taught that Christ is only *like* the Father in essence (*homoiousios*), but the council declared that Christ is the *same* substance with the Father (*homoousios*).

The letter to *Thyatira* (Rev 2:18-29) seems to picture that time known to history as the Middle Ages. From the fall of the Roman Empire until the Reformation, the Roman Catholic Church dominated medieval Europe. The word *Thyatira* means "continual sacrifice." It is the doctrine of transubstantiation, the theory accepted by Rome as a dogma in A.D. 1215, which states that the elements actually become the body and blood of Christ. If Christ is substantially present in the mass, then the sacrifice of the cross is repeated continually. Though this is still the most unique feature of the Roman Church, which sets it apart from evangelical Christianity, this facet of Romanism emerged during the time in church history covered by the letter to Thyatira.

Sardis (Rev 3:1-6) seems to cover that time just before and during the Reformation. The name means "those escaping." The church is dead; out of it escapes a remnant. This is a picture of the pre-Reformation era out of which the great Reformers come. Though the Reformation had its official beginning in 1517 when Luther nailed his ideas for debate to the church door at Wittenberg, other Reformers arose in the sixteenth century to challenge the church: Zwingli, Menno Simons, Calvin, Beza, Knox, Latimer, Cranmer. However, even before this time, other voices of dissent had been heard: Wycliffe in the fourteenth century and John Hus in the fifteenth.

Philadelphia, "brotherly love" (Rev 3:7-13), characterizes the revival church of the post-Reformation era. This time seems to have reached its peak in the eighteenth and nineteenth centuries. The church is characterized by a concern for others in missions and evangelism. There is no word of condemnation for this church. Filled with the power of the Spirit, this revival church has a door opened before it which no man can close. This church, which also represents the spiritual body of believers, will be kept from the hour of trial—the great tribulation—which is to come upon the earth (v. 10). (Contrast this with the fact that the church in Thyatira will go into the great-tribulation period, 2:22. This suggests that the true church, composed of born-again believers, will be taken out before the great tribulation begins, while the institutional and merely professing church will have a part in the tribulation. Revelation 17 confirms this, indicating that there will be an apostate form of the church upon earth after the true church, the body of Christ, has been taken out at the rapture.)

The last era of church history that will prevail until the Lord's return is characterized by the letter to *Laodicea* (Rev 3:14-22). Laodicea means "people ruling." Just as the church of the Middle Ages was a clergy-dominated church, so the church at the end of the age will be dominated by the laity. "The voice of the people is the voice of God" will be the theme of the end time of this age.

This is the church that is lukewarm and inoffensive. It is popular and inert; it exists for the people, and in turn is dominated by them. Whatever is popular and acceptable is imposed on this church. It makes God sick! (The word "spew," v. 16, means to vomit.)

So the church comes to the end of the age, not a victorious church that sweeps all before its conquest, but a church that is weak, anemic, and nauseating to the Lord. Though this is the form that the professing church will take when the age has run its course, there will be a remnant of truly born-again believers among the visible church. It is these who will be translated when Jesus comes for His own.

This brings us to the closing event of the church age—the rapture of the church. Paul says in 1 Thessalonians 4:13-18,

> But we would not have you ignorant, brethren, concerning them that fall asleep; that ye sorrow not, even as the rest, who have no hope. For if we believe that Jesus died and rose again, even so them also that are fallen asleep in Jesus will God bring with him. For this we say unto you by the word of the Lord, that we that are alive, that are left unto the coming of the Lord, shall in no wise precede them that are fallen asleep. For the Lord himself shall descend from heaven, with a shout, with the voice of the archangel, and with the trump of God: and the dead in Christ shall rise first; then we that are alive, that are left, shall together with them be caught up in the clouds, to meet the Lord in the air: and so shall we ever be with the Lord. Wherefore comfort one another with these words.

This event comes at the close of the church age and before the beginning of the tribulation period. It means that the church does not go through the tribulation. This premise recognizes the difference between Israel and the church and views the church as a mystery that intervenes between God's past and future dealing with the nation Israel. There is no evidence in any verse of Scripture that the church is in the tribulation period. The "elect" of Matthew 24:22 are not the church, but Israel. The true church is not found between Revelation 4 and 19 where the course of the tribulation period is presented. In fact, the church is promised deliverance from tribulation (1 Th 1:9-10; 5:9; cf. Rev 6:17) and therefore does not appear in the great-tribulation passages (Deu 4:29-30; Jer 30:4-11; Dan 9:24-27; Mt 24:15-31).

Only under this assumption can the return of the Lord for the church be considered an imminent coming (1 Th 1:10; 5:6; Titus 2:13). If the church is to go through the tribulation period, then there would be no reason to encourage her to watchfulness. The return of the Lord for His own could not occur at any moment, but only after certain tribulation events were fulfilled. However, the believer is encouraged to watch because the return of the Lord for His church could happen momentarily.

Not only does a pretribulation rapture of the church bring the church age to an abrupt and unannounced climax, but the imminent coming of Christ for His church recognizes the difference between His second coming and the rapture of the church. If they are not distinctively different they are at least distinguishable. The difference between these two phases of the second coming are set forth in the prophetic Scriptures as follows:

The Rapture	*The Second Coming*
1. Coming *for* His saints 2 Th 2:1	1. Coming *with* His saints Rev 19:14; Col 3:4
2. Coming in the air 1 Th 4:17	2. Coming to the earth Zec 14:3 ff.
3. Coming not public Mt 24:42 f.	3. Coming is public Rev 1:7
4. Coming is selective Mt 24:40	4. Coming is comprehensive Mt 24:31

5. Coming is a mystery
   1 Co 15:51

5. The theme of the Old
   Testament Dan 7:13

6. No signs for the rapture
   Mt 24:44

6. Many signs precede
   Mt 24:30

7. Coming is imminent
   Titus 2:13

7. Only after the tribulation Mt 24:30

8. Rewards
   Rev 22:12

8. Judgment
   Mt 25:31

Three distinctive events are to accompany the rapture of
the church. First, when Jesus returns for the church, the
dead in Christ are raised: "But we would not have you
ignorant, brethren, concerning them that fall asleep; that ye
sorrow not, even as the rest, who have no hope. For if we
believe that Jesus died and rose again, even so them also
that are fallen asleep in Jesus will God bring with him" (1 Th
4:13-14).

The fact that there will be a resurrection was well known
from the Old Testament, as was the fact that the saints of
God will come *with* Christ (Zec 14:5; Jude 14 f.). But the
fact that Christ will come first *for* His saints is a mystery, as
is the fact that when He comes for His saints, *only* the dead
"in Christ," that is, the church, will arise from the dead. The
Old Testament knew of a general resurrection. It is this new
truth, namely, that Jesus will come for His church and that
the church alone will experience a distinctive resurrection at
the rapture, apart from other of the saints of God, that Paul
calls a mystery. Therefore, the rapture is a third mystery,
along with the setting aside of Israel during the interim, and
the out-calling of the church, all three of which were unknown in the Old Testament. "Behold, I tell you a mystery:
We all shall not sleep, but we shall all be changed, in a
moment, in the twinkling of an eye, at the last trump: for the
trumpet shall sound, and the dead shall be raised incorrup-
tible, and we shall be changed" (1 Co 15:51-52).

Therefore, at the rapture of the church, every Christian who has died since the day of Pentecost will arise from the dead. Daniel speaks of a resurrection after the tribulation period (12:1-2), which has led some to believe that the church will go through the tribulation period. However, the resurrection to which Daniel refers is a resurrection that *does* take place after the tribulation period, but it is a resurrection of the Old Testament saints and *not* the church.

Second, when Jesus comes for the church, all living believers will be translated: "Then we that are alive, that are left, shall together with them be caught up in the clouds, to meet the Lord in the air: and so shall we ever be with the Lord" (1 Th 4:17). That generation of believers who are alive when the Lord returns will not experience death, but will receive resurrection bodies in a moment, in a twinkling of an eye (1 Co 15:52).

Third, the judgment seat of Christ will be set and believers will be rewarded according to works done in Jesus' name. Of course, this judgment of the believer will not determine salvation, for the issue of salvation is settled in this life (Ro 8:1; Heb 10:17; 1 Jn 4:17; Jn 5:24). But at the judgment seat of Christ the believer's works will be tested (1 Co 3:10-15). If the believer's works shall abide the test then he will receive a reward.

The exact nature of these rewards is not known, but they are called "crowns." Five such crowns are mentioned in the New Testament (1 Co 9:25; 1 Th 2:19; Ja 1:12; 2 Ti 4:8; and 1 Pe 5:4). Perhaps the real significance of these crown rewards lies in Revelation 4, where the rapture of the church is suggested by the fact that a door opens in heaven and a voice says, "Come up hither" (4:1). Before the throne that is set in heaven John sees the twenty-four elders who represent the raptured church and have received their crowns. Now watch: "The four and twenty elders shall fall down before him that sitteth on the throne, and shall worship him that liveth, for ever and ever, and shall cast their crowns before the throne" (Rev 4:10).

It will be the distinct privilege of the raptured church to receive whatever reward is due for faithful service and then to cast those crowns at Jesus' feet as a great act of worship and adoration, saying, "Worthy art thou, our Lord and our God, to receive the glory and the honor and the power: for thou didst create all things, and because of thy will they were, and were created" (Rev 4:11).

5

The Time of Israel's Tribulation

Matthew 24:9-14

THE CHURCH AGE is concluded with the gathering of the church out of the world. When the unique entity that is the church is removed, God's time clock for Israel as a nation begins to tick again. That pendulum which has hung still and unmoved for the last two thousand years will begin to swing again, to tick off the final minutes and the hours and the days that make up the seventieth week of Daniel's great time-prophecy concerning Israel. The terminal stage of God's program for Israel is designated by the three words in Matthew 24 that indicate the movement of Jesus' thought about the future of the nation Israel. As the American Standard Version translates them, these three words are: "tribulation" (vv. 9-14), "great tribulation" (vv. 15-28), and "after the tribulation" (vv. 29-31). The whole of Daniel's seventieth week is known as the tribulation period. But since Daniel divides the week into two halves, according to the time that the Antichrist breaks the covenant with Israel, in the midst of the week; we therefore call the first three and one-half years the "tribulation," and the last three and one-half years the "great-tribulation" period. This is also the terminology which Jesus uses here in Matthew 24 as He indicates the same events which divide the seventieth week.

"Then shall they deliver you up unto tribulation, and shall kill you" (v. 9). Israel had its beginning of "travail" (vv.

4-8) in that time between the death of Christ and the destruction of Jerusalem in A.D. 70. The next great event, after
the age of the church has run its course, is a time of tribulation which is to come upon Israel. It is important to notice
who in Israel is to experience tribulation during the first three
and one-half years of the period. Jesus said that at this time
it will be those who are hated of all nations "for my name's
sake" (v. 9). Obviously this must exclude unbelieving Israel
who have nothing to do with the name of Christ at the beginning of the tribulation period. In fact, it is the entire
tribulation period that gets unbelieving Israel ready to receive Jesus as Messiah. Therefore, here at the beginning of
the tribulation period, those who are hated for His name's
sake in Israel cannot be the nation as a whole. The nation is
at this time yet in unbelief.

Another reason why this cannot refer to Israel as a whole at
the beginning of the tribulation period is that the prophetic
Scriptures indicate that Israel nationally will have a little
time of peace and tranquillity during the three and one-half
years which make up the first half of the tribulation period.
During this time the Antichrist has made a covenant with
Israel and under his protection Israel prospers nationally.
But in these verses Jesus speaks of turmoil, hatred and strife.

Who then in Israel is to have tribulation at this time? Who
are these Jews who are to be persecuted for Jesus' sake? It is
the believing remnant in Israel who will accept Jesus as
Saviour at the beginning of the tribulation period.

The chronology of events seems to follow this order: Israel
is being regathered back to the land in unbelief even now
during the closing days of the church age. When the church
is raptured, all born-again believers will be caught out of the
world. However, soon after the seventieth week has begun
its course, many Jews will turn to Christ and be saved. While
Israel nationally will not recognize Jesus as Messiah until
His second coming at the close of the tribulation period, in-

dividual Jews will be saved at the beginning of the period. They are identified in the book of the Revelation as the 144,000 and, as a result of their ministry, many other Jews, as well as Gentiles, will come to know Christ as Saviour. It is this latter group of Jews, who will be saved early in the tribulation period, whom Jesus seems to have specifically in mind in verses 9-14. And it is these Jews who come to Christ and who are not among the sealed 144,000 who suffer martyrdom as a result of their allegiance to Him. Therefore, it is this saved and martyred remnant—exclusive of the 144,000— who are the subject of Jesus' words in verses 9-14. It is they who suffer "for my name's sake," Jesus said.

THREE GROUPS IN RELIGIOUS SITUATION

Soon after the rapture of the church the religious situation in Israel seems to involve *three* groups. First, there is Israel nationally which remains in unbelief during the entire tribulation period, only to accept Jesus as Messiah at the close of the period. Second, there is the 144,000 who are saved and sealed for a ministry to all the nations, as well as to Israel. Then, third, there are those Jews who are saved and who experience martyrdom as a result of their faith. It is this third group which causes the internal turmoil in Israel, hinted at in Matthew 24:10-12.

We look now at each of these three groups within Israel soon after the seventieth week of Daniel, or the tribulation period, begins.

First, there is Israel, still nationally in unbelief. Though all Jews may not be in the Holy Land during the tribulation period, it is clear that Israel is in the land and *there* the Antichrist deals with them. This is substantiated by two facts. First, Israel is in the land today; the regathering has already begun. In fact, more Jews are in Israel today than there were in the first century A.D. This regathering, the preliminaries of which we are seeing today, may continue throughout the tribulation period. (However, remember that an even more spectacular regathering will occur at Christ's second coming.)

The second thing that substantiates Israel's restoration is the Bible doctrine of scattering and regathering which will have its greatest expression at the end of the age (Deu 28:62-66; 30:1-6). The ten tribes were scattered in 721 B.C. by Assyria. Judah was scattered in 587 B.C. by Babylon. Though a remnant returned after the exile, they never found the blessings of the restoration promises because this was not the regathering that was to usher in the golden age. Israel was scattered again from off their land in A.D. 70 by the Romans. Finally, in A.D. 135 they were scattered among the nations, where a larger part remain unto this day. Only in our day have we seen the Jews returning to their promised land in significant numbers.

The Zionist movement made plans in our day to encourage the Jews to return to their ancient land. The Jews never lost their sentiment for *Eretz Israel* ("the Land of Israel"). Though Zionism—the Jewish national movement back to the land—began in eastern and central Europe in the nineteenth century, the longing to return to Palestine had been with the Jews since the Middle Ages. The love of Zion was most intense in eastern Europe because there, and particularly in Russia, the Jews were never allowed to join meaningfully in government or society. They had their own language, Yiddish, and lived in separate communities where they perpetuated their own culture and business structure. In Russia they did not have political or legal equality with other citizens.

Then, because of mid-nineteenth-century bloody repressionary measures in eastern Europe, a large-scale emigration began to western Europe and the United States, with a few returning to Palestine. One result of this return was the formation of the *Hovevei Zion* ("Lovers of Zion") movement, designed to promote the settlement of Jewish farmers and artisans in Palestine. Though these early settlements were able to survive only with the help of Baron Edmond de Rothschild of Paris, they laid the foundation for later Jewish colonization in Palestine.

Zionism found its greatest leader in Theodor Herzl, an Austrian journalist who in the pre-World War I days of the Hapsburg Émpire lived in the midst of intense anti-Semitism. He convened the first Zionist congress at Basel in August, 1897. The avowed purpose of Zionism was stated by this congress: "Zionism strives to create for the Jewish people a home in Palestine secured by public law." Though other areas of the world were to be offered to the Zionists for Jewish settlement—for example, Great Britain offered them 6,000 square miles in the highlands of Uganda in 1903—Zionism was never diverted from its main design: to create a home for the Jews in their ancient land.

Before World War I interrupted the movement, Jewish settlement in Palestine made steady progress. By 1914 there were 90,000 Jews settled in Palestine. Between the two great wars Jewish emigration continued, and by 1925 the population was estimated at 108,000. It had jumped to 300,000 by the end of 1935, with five hundred square miles owned by Jews.

But, despite this steady growth, it was not until Hitlerism and the large-scale extermination of European Jews that many Jews, especially in the United States, seriously embraced Zionism. In 1942 a Zionist conference in New York demanded the establishment of a Jewish state in Palestine with unlimited Jewish immigration. As a result of potential conflicts with Arab rights in Palestine, the issue was submitted to the United Nations. On May 14, 1948, the United Nations proclaimed the existence of the new State of Israel, which was immediately recognized by the United States.

With the establishment of the new State of Israel, all that Zionism had striven for was accomplished. But although Zionism had begun the movement back to Palestine, the Balfour Declaration, issued in Great Britain in 1917, created the climate for the establishment of the Jews in Palestine. It declared: "His Majesty's Government views with favor the establishment in Palestine of a national home for the Jewish people, and will use their best endeavours to facilitate the achievement of this object it being clearly understood that nothing shall be done which may prejudice the civil and religious rights of existing non-Jewish communities in Palestine, or the rights and political status enjoyed by Jews in any other country."

During World War I, the British army, under the command of General Allenby, had liberated Palestine from the Turks in 1917. In 1922 the League of Nations approved a British mandate over Palestine which included the Balfour Declaration in its preamble. That declaration probably did more than anything else to influence both British and American thinking about the Jews in the Middle East, and led to the time when the State of Israel would be finally achieved. When the British withdrew from the new State of Israel in 1948, the Jewish population had risen to 650,000. By 1960 it had reached almost two million. At the beginning of 1971 the total Jewish population was 2,560,000. Of this total, 45.1 percent are native born. The rest came as immigrants: 28:1 percent from Europe and the United States; 14.2 percent from Africa; and 12.6 percent from Asia.[1]

Though the Jewish population in Israel today numbers more than the Jewish population of Jesus' day, these Jews are there in unbelief. However, this too is according to the prophetic Word. Deuteronomy 30:3-6 says,

> Then Jehovah thy God will turn thy captivity, and have compassion upon thee, and will return and gather thee from all the peoples, whither Jehovah thy God hath scattered thee. If any of thine outcasts be in the uttermost parts of heaven,

[1]Figures are based upon those given in *Facts About Israel* (Jerusalem: Keter Books, 1971).

> from thence will Jehovah thy God gather thee, and from thence will he fetch thee: and Jehovah thy God will bring thee into the land which thy fathers possessed, and thou shalt possess it; and he will do thee good, and multiply thee above thy fathers. And Jehovah thy God will circumcise thy heart, and the heart of thy seed, to love Jehovah thy God with all thy heart, and with all thy soul, that thou mayest live.

Notice that the circumcision of heart which will cause them to love the Lord will occur *after* they have been regathered. Ezekiel predicts the same thing, in the same sequence:

> For I will take you from among the nations, and gather you out of all the countries, and will bring you into your own land. And I will sprinkle clean water upon you, and ye shall be clean: from all your filthiness, and from all your idols, will I cleanse you. A new heart also will I give you, and a new spirit will I put within you. . . . And I will put my Spirit within you, and cause you to walk in my statutes, and ye shall keep mine ordinances, and do them (36:24-27).

Again notice that the spiritual renewal comes *after* they are regathered back into the land and not before. And incidentally, this transformation did not happen after the return from the Babylonian exile, and therefore must refer to a future regathering which results in spiritual renewal.

Religion plays an important part in the tribulation period. In fact, it will be one of the most "religious" periods of the earth's history. For this reason Jesus warns, "And many false prophets shall arise, and shall lead many astray" (Mt 24: 11). The religious condition in unbelieving Israel during the first half of the tribulation period will be familiar because they will return to the Old Testament Levitical system of priesthood and offerings.

It is interesting that all the temple treasures that could be found—the temple menorah (the seven-armed lamp), the table of showbread, the garments of the priest, the silver trumpets sounded at the morning and evening sacrifice—were all taken to Rome and displayed for its citizens when Jerusalem was captured by Titus in A.D. 70. A magnificent arch, on which the menorah was carved, was erected in the Roman Forum to commemorate Titus' victory over the Jews. But the actual lampstand and other temple treasures were deposited in the Roman Temple of Peace, except for the scrolls of the law and the curtain from the holy of holies which were carefully kept in the imperial palace.

But what ultimately happened to the temple treasures? When Rome fell to the invading barbarians, they disappeared. One report says they were cast into the Tiber River when in 312 Constantine conquered the city. Another story says they were taken along with other treasures by the Vandals in 544 when they sacked the city. However, a third tradition says they are still hidden in Constantinople where they were brought after the Vandal kingdom was defeated. Who knows, these very vestments and instruments may be recovered and used again in the temple worship!

There is also much tradition concerning the ark of the covenant which disappeared from the first temple. The Babylonian Talmud records that Rabbi Eliezer said, "The ark went into exile in Babylon" (Yoma 53b-54a). The rabbis also believed that 2 Chronicles 36:10 and Isaiah 39:6 taught that the ark went to Babylon. There is another Jewish legend to the effect that the ark was hidden in the temple area where the wood for the sacrificial fires was kept. A certain priest while working there one day noticed that some of the stones in the paved floor projected above the others. He had no sooner begun to tell the story to another priest when he fell dead. This was regarded as a sure sign that the ark was buried there (Yer. Shek. 6:49c).

However, the Apocrypha records that the prophet Jeremiah hid the ark just before the Babylonians came:

The prophet, being warned of God, commanded the tabernacle and the ark to go with him, as he went forth into the mountain, where Moses climbed up, and saw the heritage of God. And when Jeremiah came thither, he found an hollow cave, wherein he laid the tabernacle, and the ark, and the altar of incense, and so stopped the door. And some of those that followed him came to mark the way, but they could not find it. Which when Jeremiah perceived, he blamed them, saying, As for that place, it shall be unknown until the time that God gather his people again together, and receive them unto mercy (2 Macc 2:4-7).

This sacred part of the Levitical system may still be hidden somewhere in Palestine and may be rediscovered and used again as the center of the temple worship during the tribulation!

Probably all the ceremonies of the Old Testament, which have not been observed since the last sacrifice was offered in the temple in midsummer of A.D. 70, will again be reinstituted. Just after the destruction of Jerusalem, the rabbis began recording in accurate detail all the temple services so their descendants would be able to resume them when the time came. Obviously the Levitical sacrifices will be reinstituted, for when the Antichrist breaks the covenant with Israel in the midst of the seventieth week of Daniel (9:27), he will "cause the sacrifice and the oblation to cease" (cf. 12:11). If they are made to cease, they will have to be started sometime previously. This infers that the temple will be rebuilt early in the tribulation period. These sacrifices can be offered in only one place (Deu 12:5-7); that is on Mount Moriah, the sacred spot where Abraham prepared to offer up Isaac, and where the temple of Solomon was located (2 Ch 3:1).

Since the fall of the temple in A.D. 70, Jews have prayed each day for its restoration. During the Middle Ages they often wore black to remind themselves that they were "mourners of Zion." Even today at weddings a Jewish bride-groom will crush a glass beneath his heel to remind everyone, even in the midst of their joy, of the temple's destruction.

There were ancient attempts to rebuild the temple after the fall of Jerusalem. Though the Midrash almost always refers to the Roman emperor Hadrian with a curse ("Hadrian, may his bones be cursed!"), in his early career he may have been friendly toward the Jews. Jewish tradition has it that he even issued a decree that the temple should be rebuilt (Gen. Rabbah 64). A passage in *The Epistle of Barnabas* (16:4) also reflects this belief that the temple was to be rebuilt about this time, for it denounces the Jews for expecting the pagan Romans to build a physical temple.

Evidently the Jews had begun collecting money for rebuilding the temple: "Pappos and Luliani, the heroes of the last revolt, set up exchange tables in Galilee and Syria, from Acco to Antioch, and provided with gold, silver and other articles those who were coming into the country from the exile" (Gen. Rabbah 64). Some rabbis interpret this passage to mean that the pilgrims could change here for Palestinian money the coins that they were bringing to Jerusalem for the reconstruction of the temple.

The rabbis even began to raise certain religious questions about the reconditioning of the temple site. These questions, called *Halakhie,* are reflected in the Mishnah and Tosefta. But all was useless because Hadrian soon withdrew his promise to rebuild. In fact, after the revolt of Bar Kokhbah was put down, Hadrian had the temple site "plowed over" and erected a temple to Jupiter with a statue of himself inside.

Julian the Apostate (A.D. 360-63), who followed Constantine upon the throne of the Roman Empire, had ordered the Jews to rebuild the temple in his day. In response, hundreds of Jews came to the city for the sacred task, and axes and spades of silver were provided by the wealthy. The Jews rejoiced and sang as they dug into the holy spot. Christian tradition says the work was periodically halted by an earthquake, a mysterious fire, and the sign of the cross appearing upon the garments of the workmen, causing some to believe in Christ and abandon their work. However, what really stopped the work was Julian's death six months after the project was started. A Christian emperor, Valentinian I (A.D. 364-75), succeeded him, and the Jews were again forbidden to enter Jerusalem. On May 20, A.D. 614, the Persians took Jerusalem. Thousands of Christians were massacred, and the survivors were expelled from the city. Again the Jews were given the freedom of the city by its Persian conquerors. The temple site was at least cleared and sacrifices may have begun after a lapse of five hundred years. But after three years, in order to placate the Christian majority in Syria, the Jews were ordered out of Jerusalem by the Persians.

In 629 the Byzantines drove the Persians out of Palestine. However, Byzantine dominion in Jerusalem was in turn soon taken over by the Caliph Omar, the successor to the successor of Muhammad. When the Byzantines surrendered Jerusalem to the caliph, he was conducted into the city to worship at the temple site, which had had no building on it since the temple of Jupiter built by Hadrian had been overturned by Christians. The spot was covered by filth, for the city's Christian inhabitants had emptied their slop pails there as an act of disrespect. According to one report, jars of excrement were especially brought from Constantinople to be unloaded there as a token of contempt for the Jews. (The Arabs used the area around the Wailing Wall similarly before the June, 1967, war, so filth had to be removed before Jews could worship there).

The caliph had to crawl on his hands and knees to enter the temple area. But the area was soon cleared, following Omar's example of tossing trash over the temple enclosure to the valley below, and the sacred rock was exposed. A simple wooden structure was built there by the Arabs to cover the rock. But within fifty years the pavement Herod had built on top of the temple mound became a place of Muslim worship and the Caliph Abd el-Malik completed the dome that stands today on the sacred spot. The exterior walls were of white marble, and the dome was covered with gold. All but the gray mass of the rock itself was covered with brightly colored mosaics. Surrounding the rock were two circles of columns, many of which were a part of the original temple of Jupiter built by the Romans. Others were carried from a ruined Byzantine church on the Mount of Olives. The Dome of the Rock has covered the sacred spot where the temple once stood from that day until this.

Today there are many rumors of Jewish intent to rebuild the temple. But how it is to be rebuilt on this sacred spot remains to be seen. Its construction will probably not get under way in our day for three reasons: First, even though the temple area was liberated from the Arabs in the Six-Day War in 1967, nevertheless, the Dome of the Rock, which now covers the sacred spot, is one of the most sacred of Islamic shrines. It is unlikely that the Arabs—backed by world opinion—would tolerate any tampering with the sacred shrine, even though it is now in Israeli territory. Second, Reformed Jews see no need for the temple. Third, most Orthodox Jews believe that the Messiah will rebuild the temple when He comes. Therefore, neither Reformed nor Orthodox Jews now have any incentive to support such a project. Apparently Jewish opinion will change when the tribulation has begun and the temple, along with its system of sacrifices and offerings, will be revived.

Therefore, the fact that the temple will be rebuilt is rather certain, for not only will the Jews reinstate the Levitical system in it during the first half of the tribulation, but the Antichrist will place his figure in it during the *last* half of the period (Dan 12:11; Mt 24:15; cf. Rev 13:15).

Though the ancient Levitical system will be one of the dominant religious forces during the first three and one-half years of the tribulation period, another important religious movement—the gospel—influences many in Israel. At the same time that ancient patterns of temple worship are reinstituted in Israel, there will also be those who will preach the gospel during the first part of the tribulation period. They are spoken of in Revelation 7 as the 144,000 who are sealed out of the tribes of Israel—12,000 out of each tribe. Though their ministry begins during the first part of the tribulation period, they seem to continue into the last three and one-half years of the great tribulation as well, for the Antichrist has no power to harm them (Rev 9:4; 14:1). It is they who will preach the gospel of the kingdom to the ends of the earth (Mt 24:14).

These words of Jesus, "And this gospel of the kingdom shall be preached to the whole world for a testimony unto all the nations; and then shall the end come," have been misapplied to the church age as if it were a sign to the church for Christ's second coming. However, in the chronology of the prophetic discourse, this must apply to the 144,000 Jewish missionaries who will preach during the tribulation and win many to Christ during that time. The fact that the end comes after they have spread the gospel of the kingdom to all nations suggests that they will be active in evangelizing the world during the whole seven-year period.

What is the nature of the saving experience during the tribulation period? If the Holy Spirit is taken out of the world, along with the church at the rapture (2 Th 2:7-8), how can the saving experience take place within individuals during the tribulation? The answer is that tribulation saints will be saved, after the Spirit is removed, in exactly the same way that people were saved before the Spirit came at Pentecost. After all, the saving ministry of the Spirit, which baptizes (1 Co 12:12-13), indwells (1 Co 6:19), seals (Eph 1:

13), and fills (Eph 5:18) is unique to our age. All these
things depend upon the indwelling presence of the Holy
Spirit within the believer. The evidence is that this distinctive and unique ministry of the Spirit to the church will
cease on earth after the rapture.

However, God has always justified the sinner by faith, even
from the time of Abraham. This phase of the redeeming experience will continue through the tribulation period. Just
as God justified the sinner by faith in Old Testament times,
during the tribulation period the sinner will also be justified
by faith. The only difference will be that of faith's perspective. In Old Testament times faith looked forward to the
cross. In the tribulation period faith will look backward to
the cross. This would mean that the relationship of the Holy
Spirit to the redeemed during the tribulation period would
be the same as His relationship to the redeemed in the Old
Testament. He came *upon* them to empower them for specific needs, but did not universally dwell *within,* as He does
now in the church.

The gospel that is to be preached during the tribulation
period is the "gospel of the kingdom" (Mt 24:14). This is
the message of John the Baptist which had two essentials:
repentance, (Mt 3:2) and beholding the Lamb (Jn 1:29; cf.
Rev 7:14; 12:11). Therefore, the message of the 144,000 during the tribulation period will be: "Repent! And behold the
Lamb of God which taketh away the sin of the world." When
a response of repentance and beholding the Lamb in faith is
made, the sinner, whether Jew or Gentile, is justified by that
faith.

The 144,000 constitute a distinctive group of the redeemed
because they cannot be harmed by the Antichrist during this
time. He would like to stop their preaching of the gospel of
the kingdom, but he cannot. As a result of their preaching
there will be numbers of people, both Jews and Gentiles,
saved during the tribulation period. Many of them will be

martyred, especially during the great tribulation. John pictures them in Revelation 7:13-17:

> And one of the elders answered, saying unto me, These that are arrayed in the white robes, who are they, and whence came they? And I say unto him, My lord, thou knowest. And he said to me, These are they that come out of the great tribulation, and they washed their robes, and made them white in the blood of the Lamb. Therefore are they before the throne of God; and they serve him day and night in his temple: and he that sitteth on the throne shall spread his tabernacle over them. They shall hunger no more, neither thirst any more; neither shall the sun strike upon them, nor any heat: for the Lamb that is in the midst of the throne shall be their shepherd, and shall guide them unto fountains of waters of life: and God shall wipe away every tear from their eyes.

This then is the group of saints who will suffer death for their faith during the tribulation period. They are the converts of the 144,000, and the group to which Jesus refers in Matthew 24:9-14 as those who will suffer for His name's sake. They shall be delivered up and hated—hated by other Jews who remain in unbelief. It is interesting that Jews who espouse Judaism have been persecuted by Christians for many centuries. The only time that Jews persecuted Christians was early in the first century. However, once again the saints of God will be the subject of Jewish persecution—as well as that of the Antichrist's hostility which will grow most intense during the latter half of the seventieth week. Because of this persecution, "the love of the many shall wax cold. But he that endureth to the end, the same shall be saved" (24: 12-13. Not necessarily the end of the tribulation period is meant, but the end of one's life. Indications are that, excepting the 144,000, those who repent and believe in the Lamb will soon suffer martyrdom for their faith.

RELIGIOUS CONDITIONS

As we attempt to give an account of the religious conditions during the first half of the seventieth week of Daniel,
we must remember that the Gentiles also have a vital role to
play in the religion of the era. They are not devoid of an institutional expression of religious faith during this period.
Revelation 17 indicates that a great apostate church will
thrive during this time.

Chronologically, Revelation 17 is in the last half of the
tribulation period; however, what is pictured there concerning the conflict between the Antichrist and the apostate
church—the woman sitting upon a scarlet-colored beast—has
its beginnings early in the tribulation period. It is then that
the great apostate church grows in power and influence. In
fact, the Antichrist during his rise to world dominion seems
to tolerate the apostate church as an instrument of his rise
to power. When he no longer needs its support, he will turn
upon it and destroy it during the last half of the period.

Ecclesiastical Babylon, or the great apostate church, is the
final fruition of the religious mania for ecumenicalism and
church union today. Just as now the stage for tribulation
events is being set in other areas, so here also. For decades
liberal theologians have been preaching church union and
striving for one great ecclesiastical monolith. During the first
part of the tribulation period, after the true church has been
raptured, their dream will be realized.

John sees this great apostate church under the figure of a
woman, a harlot, sitting astride a scarlet-colored beast (Rev
17:2 ff.). Women in the book of the Revelation represent
religion; see Revelation 2:20 where a woman, Jezebel, represents pagan religion; and Revelation 12:1, where Israel is
represented by a woman. The true church is also under the
representation of a woman, the bride (Rev 19:7 f.; 21:9; Eph
5:25). This woman astride the beast is to the Antichrist what

the true church is to Jesus Christ. For in the tribulation not only is there a counterfeit trinity composed of Satan (acting as God), Antichrist (acting as Jesus), and the false prophet (acting as the Holy Spirit), but there is also a counterfeit church, ecclesiastical Babylon.

It is the apostate church, symbolized by the woman who is a harlot, which is in league with the Antichrist. This is why she is pictured sitting astride the beast (17:3, 7). Later, when the apostate church is no longer needed, the harlot is destroyed (v. 16). But during the first part of the tribulation period the apostate church and the Antichrist arise together, each contributing to the influence and power of the other. The fact that the woman is a harlot (v. 1) suggests this church's apostate nature. This figure is used throughout the Old Testament to signify the defection to idolatry (Jer 3:6, 8; Is 1:21; cf. Ja 4:4-5).

Though the true church will not be in the tribulation, some form of an institutional church will be in existence during this time. What is its form and origin? Philadelphia, the spiritual church (Rev 3:10) will not be in the tribulation, but the church of Thyatira will (Rev 2:22). This church represents the Roman Catholic Church of the Middle Ages. The structure of the Roman Church will persist into the tribulation, forming the framework of the apostate church.

Truly born-again believers in the Roman communion will be raptured when the Lord comes for His own before the tribulation begins. However, since the Roman Church has never clearly understood the terms of salvation by faith alone, nor preached them uncompromisingly, many of its members have not been born again. Though this is also the case among some Protestant churches, it is most evident in the Roman Church which has perverted the simple terms of salvation by the addition of works, sacraments, indulgences, the mass, and the worship of Mary. Therefore, the Roman Church will form the outward structure of the apostate world church of the tribulation period.

Too much in the picture of the great harlot smacks of the worst of Romanism for this not to be the case. Consider, for example, that the harlot sits upon many waters (17:1). Verse 15 interprets this as people. Here is a picture that has had its counterpart in every South American and European country where the Roman Church dominates government. There has always been an immoral union between Romanism and government. Note that this is suggested in the fact that the kings of the earth commit fornication with her (v. 2) in a wilderness (v. 3). The Roman Church has always thrived in a spiritual wilderness. When spiritual religion thrives, then revival and reformation occur—but not here. She is decked (Gk: gilded) with fine array (v. 4). The more a church loses a sense of inner values and spirituality, the more it depends on outward pomp and show. This has always characterized Romanism; she is drunken with the blood of the saints (v. 6). There has always been a tendency in the Roman Church to solve the problem of alternative belief by murdering those who hold it. During the tribulation all the horrors of the days of the inquisitions will be revived, and the Roman Church, which modern civilization has intimidated into tolerating the faith of others, will once again turn in wrath upon those who disagree with her.

POLITICAL CONDITIONS

These, then, are the religious circumstances at the beginning of the tribulation period. But what about political conditions? Certain world events of a political nature revolve around the meteoric rise of one figure, the Antichrist. As this sinister figure emerges from the Mediterranean area he will at first dominate the countries that make up the boundaries of the old Roman Empire. Then he will step from this to world dominion. All this will occur during the first three and one-half years of the tribulation period. Arriving at world dominion, he will then be unmasked as the beast of Revelation 13, and all the horrors of the great tribulation will be unloosed upon Israel. However, here we will trace his rise during the first half of the seventieth week as he emerges as a new Roman Caesar and then becomes a world dictator.

Chronologically, Revelation 6 provides the first picture of the tribulation events just after the rapture of the church. The first four seals view a time of bloodless conquest, followed by war, along with its aftermath of famine and death. These are the events that surround the early rise of the Antichrist that makes him a new Caesar, head of a ten-nation confederation which is a revived form of the ancient Roman Empire.

The first four seals that are broken present four different horses. Only the horses differ, not the rider, for he is the same person—the Antichrist who rides to prominence upon these four disasters. The first, pictured by the white horse (Rev 6:1-2), is that of bloodless conquest. Jesus rides a white horse in His world conquest at His second coming (Rev 19: 11), but it is the Antichrist who comes upon the world scene at this point. It is a time of bloodless conquest, suggested by the bow but no arrows (v. 2). Antichrist will take a crown and rule as a result of this conquest. Then he will offer to bring order out of the chaotic events which will have resulted from the church having just vacated the world. It takes little imagination to envision what confusion will result when suddenly all Christians are gone from the earth. This may be the resulting world confusion that is described when the sixth seal is broken (Rev 6:12-17). The great upheaval may be political, religious, economic and social, in which all stability is lost—a perfect condition in which a strong leader can emerge.

The Antichrist soon faces opposition, however. This is suggested by the next horse, which is red (6:3-4). He takes a sword of war in order to complete his rise to power and to secure his hold upon the territory over which he rides. This is also suggested in Daniel (7:8, 20) in which three horns must be plucked up before the little horn—the Antichrist—is fully established in his dominion over all the ten horns.

The third seal presents a black horse (6:5-6). This represents the inevitable famine and starvation which follow war. As has happened so often in past history, this also creates a condition conducive to the rise of a strong figure who will promise a solution to the suffering and privation which many are enduring. As a result of the famine and starvation, death, represented by the pale horse (6:7-8), rides forth.

All these ingredients together promote the spectacular rise of the Antichrist as leader of ten confederated nations early in the tribulation period. At this time he gives evidence of being able to create order out of chaos and of becoming a great benefactor of mankind caught in the spiritual void resulting from the rapture of the church and the removal of all spiritual influences from the earth. He is not seen as the Satan-inspired egomaniac who later in the great tribulation period will demand absolute submission to his will and the pagan worship of his person. For now, he is a figure who offers solutions to world problems of economics, international tensions, and perhaps even religious perplexities, due to the sudden translation of the church. The fact that he has some relation to Judaism and also the apostate world church indicates that his rise to power has religious connotations as well as political.

But why is the first area of the Antichrist's conquest assumed to be a revived form of the ancient Roman Empire? To answer this we must return to Daniel's two visions that previewed the times of the Gentiles. In Daniel 2 and 7 the prophet sees four great world empires that will come upon the scene of history and which will constitute the context of the Gentiles' treading down Jerusalem (Lk 21:24).

The first is the Babylonian Empire, represented by the head of gold in Daniel's first vision (2:36-38) and by a lion in his second vision (7:4). The fall of Babylon occurred on the night of October 13, 539 B.C., a decade after Cyrus had effected a union between the Medes and the Persians (549 B.C.). This second world empire, the Medo-Persian, is symbolized by the breast and arms of silver in Daniel 2:39a, and by a bear raised up on one side with three ribs in his mouth (7:5). The fact that the bear is raised up on one side may suggest the imbalance of Persian power over Media. The three ribs in his mouth may suggest the main constituencies of the empire: Media, Persia and Babylon. In another vision, Daniel sees the Medo-Persian Empire as a ram (Dan 8:3-4; cf. v. 20). In this latter vision the emphasis is upon the empire's swift expansion (8:4).

A third world empire soon follows. By this time Daniel is looking two hundred years into the future where he sees the rise of the Greek Empire, represented in his first vision by the belly and thighs of brass (2:39). Here the extent of Greek dominion is noted as being greater geographically than the two previous kingdoms.

In his second vision, Daniel sees the Greek Empire under the figure of a leopard with four wings and four heads (7:6). Alexander the Great defeated the Persians in three great moves: the Battle of Granicus, 334 B.C.; the Battle of Issus, 333 B.C.; and the Battle of Gaugamela, 331 B.C. When Alexander came to Palestine in 331 B.C., the city of Jerusalem yielded to him without protest. The amazing story of this event is related by Josephus.[1]

When Alexander died in 323 B.C., his empire was divided among four of his generals. This is pictured in another of Daniel's visions in 8:8. It is also suggested by the fact that the leopard in his second vision had four heads and wings. One of Alexander's generals, Ptolemy, was given Egypt. The

[1]Josephus, *Antiquities*, 11:8.

Ptolemaic rule in Egypt was extended to Palestine and lasted there from 320 B.C. until 198 B.C. when it passed to Syria, which had been given to another of Alexander's generals, Seleucid. It was out of the Seleucid rule in Palestine that Antiochus Epiphanes, who is a type of the Antichrist (cf. 8:9 ff.), terrorized the countryside, desecrated the temple, and fomented the Jewish civil war which gave the Jews a brief respite from Gentile control.

However, this relief did not last, for Daniel sees a fourth world empire more terrible than all the rest. This is the Roman Empire which is pictured in his first vision by the legs of iron and the feet partly of iron and clay (2:40-45). It is important to note how Daniel views the last of these world empires. First, it is divided into two parts, suggested by the legs. This happened when Constantine moved his capital to the Greek city of Byzantium on the Black Sea in A.D. 330 and renamed it Constantinople (now Istanbul). This transfer of the capital from Rome to the east meant a division of the empire. Though this was the beginning of the long history of the Byzantine Empire, from that time on the history of the old Roman Empire was one of weakness and decay.

Gradually the barbarians from the north in Europe came down into Italy, and in A.D. 410 Alaric captured Rome. After that the Roman Empire was invaded by wave after wave of Goths, Huns, Lombards and Vandals. Romulus Augustulus, whose name contained the name of Rome's legendary founder and that of the empire's first emperor, was the last ruler of the western division. He was deposed in A.D. 476 by the barbarian leader, Odoacer. The Roman Empire was at an end, say the history books.

But was it? Daniel's vision continues as he sees a further division, suggested by the feet and ten toes (Dan 2:42 ff.). From our standpoint this is prophecy and not history, for what Daniel sees concerning the feet and ten toes has never been fulfilled:

> And in the days of those kings [represented by the ten
> toes] shall the God of heaven set up a kingdom which shall
> never be destroyed, nor shall the sovereignty thereof be left
> to another people; but it [the kingdom that God shall es-
> tablish in the days of those kings] shall break in pieces and
> consume all those kingdoms, and it shall stand for ever. For-
> asmuch as thou sawest that a stone was cut out of the moun-
> tain without hands, and that it brake in pieces the iron, the
> brass, the clay, the silver, and the gold; the great God hath
> made known to the king what shall come to pass hereafter
> (2:44-45).

What is Daniel saying? That the kingdom, represented by
the feet and toes, will be in existence when the second coming of Christ occurs! This means that some form of the old
Roman Empire which passed from the pages of history fifteen
hundred years ago must be revived in the last days before the
times of the Gentiles end.

This idea that the Roman Empire will live again is not without some historical precedent, however. The spirit of Rome
has already had a revival once before in history, after a thousand years in abeyance. This revival is known to history as
the Renaissance. The culture of the Middle Ages was a faith-
oriented culture, but the Renaissance was a rebirth of interest
in the past. The glories of classical antiquity caused the
Renaissance man to seek the wisdom of the ancient world and
especially that of Rome. In matters of science he returned
to Aristotle for physics and to Galen for medicine. The language of Rome was Latin, which was eulogized as "the sweet-
est, richest and most cultured" of all languages. Latin litera-
ture, along with Greek ideals, became the basis of classical
education. In politics and law, one was encouraged to "think
like a Roman."

The desire to learn from the Roman caused men of the
Renaissance to study principally the historians, men like Livy
and Tacitus. Quintilian and Cicero's theories on education

and on the qualities of character which best met the challenge of the Roman world were also adjusted to meet the Renaissance world of the fourteenth and fifteenth centuries. In short, the Renaissance, with no concept of evolutionary progress in social, economic, political or scientific thought, did not develop the belief that man could improve society by discovery of new methods of organizing life, but believed that the ancient world of the Romans held the key to the proper structure of society. Hence, they were determined to rediscover rather than invent. They felt they could improve man's position, not by looking forward to new discoveries, as we do, but by looking backward. To them the ancient world had done everything about as well as it could be done. Society therefore must learn again the precepts laid down by the Romans.

This revival occurred on the northern shore of the Mediterranean Sea on the site where the ancient Roman Empire began. It was a revival of the very spirit of Rome. Paggio Bracciolini, one of the greatest Renaissance scholars, viewing the centuries of calloused neglect of the ancient capital, said that Rome "now lies prostrate like a great corpse, decayed, and everywhere eaten away." But it was this very city that became the fountainhead of the cultural revival known as the Renaissance. After a thousand years of the dark ages, the Roman Empire was reborn in the spirit of the Italian Renaissance. Anything that dynamic can revive once again!

However, only once did a Renaissance ruler try to revive the ancient Roman Empire politically. It was in 1347 that Cola di Rienzo seized the Roman government and reclaimed the ancient title of "Tribune of the People." He tried to entice all Italy into a federation of states, but the time was not right for the empire to revive politically. This will happen during the tribulation. During the Renaissance the interest in ancient Rome was cultural and not political. Giovanni Villani, a Florentine historian, said, "Rienzo wanted to bring all

Italy under the obedience of Rome in the way of long ago"; but, said he, "the enterprise was fantastic and could not endure." And so it could not then. But it will one day! If the spirit of Rome could live again in the Renaissance after a thousand years had swept over its grave, then it is not unthinkable to believe that Rome will live again politically during the tribulation period.

In chapter 2 Daniel views the ancient Roman Empire up to verse 40; then, as do all the Old Testament prophets, he does not see the age of the church—or the great parenthesis, as we have called it—intruding between verses 40 and 41. He therefore moves from a description of the ancient Roman Empire to a description of the revived Roman Empire of the last days, suggested by the ten toes of 2:41 and the ten horns of 7:7, 20, passing unseen over the age of the church, which is the valley between these two mountain peaks of history.

In his second vision in 7:7-28, Daniel sees the same thing. In verse 7 he describes the ancient Roman Empire. But toward the end of the verse his vision passes over the age of the church and he is speaking of the time of the end, beginning with the words, "and it had ten horns." Verse 8 and the following verses are a picture of the revived Roman Empire made up of a ten-nation confederation. As in his first vision, Daniel beholds until the second coming of Christ occurs (vv. 9-14).

Again, it is imperative to note that the establishment of God's kingdom, ushered in by Christ's second coming, occurs when the final form of the fourth empire is in existence. Since the historical Roman Empire passed out of existence centuries ago, we must posit a revived form of that empire in the closing days of the times of the Gentiles. This ten-nation confederation, suggested by the ten toes of the image in Daniel's first vision and the ten horns subdued by the little horn in his second vision, will probably occupy the boundaries of the ancient Roman Empire. It is out of this revived form of the Roman Empire that the Antichrist arises.

Daniel also pictures this in his second vision (7:20-21). As he contemplates the ten horns—the revived Roman Empire composed of a ten-nation confederation—a little horn arises. This little horn, full of eyes, "and a mouth that spake great things, whose look was more stout than its fellows," is the Antichrist. His conquest involves the subduing of three horns (v. 20). Apparently early in the tribulation period the Antichrist struggles with three of the nations that are found within the geographical bounds of the ancient Roman Empire. They fall to his conquest. The rest apparently yield to him without a struggle. This is consistent with what Revelation 6 says in the appearance of both the white horse and the red horse, that is, a bloodless conquest and war.

These seem to be the conditions during the first half of the seventieth week of Daniel, or the time of *tribulation,* as Jesus calls it in His great prophetic discourse in Matthew 24. Religiously there are three groups: (1) unbelieving Israel, which reinstitutes the Levitical system of worship; (2) the great apostate world church, which thrives because of the patronage of the new Roman Caesar, the Antichrist (just as the ancient Roman Catholic Church thrived because of the patronage of another Roman Caesar); and (3) the 144,000 Jewish missionaries and their converts. This latter group will suffer persecution and it is to them that Jesus addresses His remarks in Matthew 24:9-14.

Since religion plays a vital part in the rise of the Antichrist, he must use these groups to his advantage. Judaism is used as the Antichrist makes a covenant with Israel during the first three and one-half years, which apparently unites all the unbelieving Jews behind his cause. When he no longer needs their support, the covenant is broken at midtribulation. He also needs the support of the apostate church. Just as the Roman Church historically has kept many a corrupt form of government in power in Europe, so in the tribulation the support of the apostate church is needed in the early days of the Antichrist's struggle for power. When he no longer needs the support of the church, he will also turn upon it and destroy it (Rev 17:16).

However, his relationship to the other group, the 144,000 and the saints who receive Christ at their preaching, is quite different. He cannot use them because they will not be subverted to his sinister ambitions, so he will persecute this group from the very first. Though he will not be able to harm the 144,000 (Rev 9:4; 14:1), he will martyr the rest of the saints (Dan 7:21; 8:24; Rev 6:9-11; 7:13-17).

6

The Time of Israel's Great Tribulation

Matthew 24:15-28

"FOR *then* shall be great tribulation, such as hath not been from the beginning of the world until now, no, nor ever shall be" (Mt 24:21). When shall there be great tribulation? When is the "then" of verse 21? Verse 15 indicates the event which will mark the beginning of the great-tribulation period, or the last three and one-half years of Daniel's seventieth week. The dramatic events begin when the Antichrist places his image in the temple and demands that it be worshiped: "*When* therefore ye see the abomination of desolation, which was spoken of through Daniel the prophet, standing in the holy place . . . *then* shall be great tribulation" (24:15-21). The "when" of verse 15 and the "then" of verse 21 stand in cause-and-effect relationship. The contents of verses 16-20 are only the correlaries of the main event that signals the start of the great-tribulation period.

RELIGIOUS OPPOSITION

At this point the Antichrist has no more use for either Judaism or the apostate church in his plans for world dominion. He crushes the great apostate world church: "And the ten horns which thou sawest, and the beast, these shall hate the harlot, and shall make her desolate and naked, and shall eat her flesh, and shall burn her utterly with fire. For God did put in their hearts to do his mind, and to come to one mind, and to give their kingdom unto the beast, until the words of God should be accomplished" (Rev 17:16-17).

The writer of the book of the Revelation has a philosophy of history—even history in its prophetic form as it was then from John's standpoint—which sees God behind all the events of the end time. In the middle of the period, the Antichrist, in order that he might have no rivals in his ultimate desire to be worshiped as a god—just as Caesar desired to be worshiped as a god—does away with the apostate church. He has used it; now it is in his way, so he destroys it.

The ecumenical movement which emerged in the twentieth century, and which creates the psychology for the great world apostate church, then comes to an end. Having begun before the rapture of the true church, the ecumenical psychology creates a ready climate for the formation of the world church of the tribulation period. And just as the great hulking institutional church of the Middle Ages was often used to further the political ambitions of the papal state, so the Antichrist has used this ecclesiastical monolith as a stepping-stone to political dominion.

Apparently those who have been a part of this great apostate church simply transfer their spiritual allegiance to the Antichrist and make him an object of their worship (Rev 13: 12). Not only have they been preconditioned to make this transfer because of the liberal psychology which characterizes the ecumenical movement and does not insist on a firm doctrinal stand about much of anything, thus making a change of gods less than traumatic, but they are also threatened with death if they do not submit to the Antichrist (Rev 13:15).

Judaism, which also enjoyed the Antichrist's tolerance during the first three and one-half years of his rise to power, now suffers at his hands. In the midst of the week, Daniel says the firm covenant is broken (9:27). As a result the sacrifices and oblations cease, which indicates that the temple rituals of the Levitical system can no longer be practiced.

This is reminiscent of the days of Antiochus Epiphanes in the second century B.C. when he too ordered the sacrifices in the temple to cease. Because Judaism was a threat to his Hellenistic designs to force Greek culture upon the Jews, Antiochus issued a royal edict requiring the Jews to worship the Hellenistic gods. He formally dedicated the Jewish temple in Jerusalem to Zeus, the supreme god of the Olympus, and offered swine's flesh as a sacrifice upon the altar (cf. 2 Macc 6:1 ff.). "It is the abomination of desolation," cried the Jews as they fled the temple where the altar of Zeus, and probably his image as well, had been erected.

The events that follow this edict of Antiochus in 168 B.C. are filled with stories of horror and cruelty suffered by the Jews who remained faithful to the law. Two mothers who had circumcised their babies in obedience to the law of Moses had them tied to their breasts, and after being paraded through the city, were cast down from the walls (2 Macc 6: 10). Another group of Jews was caught observing the Sabbath and the entire group was burned (2 Macc 6:11). Eleazar, a noted scribe, was forced to eat pork. He spat it out and was beaten to death (2 Macc 6:18-31).

One of the most famous stories that comes out of this period when Antiochus Epiphanes ruled in Palestine is that of seven brothers and their mother who refused to eat swine's flesh and who were tormented and beaten. As the mother and brothers watched, one son was taken and his tongue cut out; then he was fried to death in a great pan over a fire. The second son was skinned and burned to death. In like manner, all seven brothers were tortured to death rather than reject the law of God. While dying, the seventh son said, "I will not obey the king's commandment: but I will obey the commandment of the law that was given unto our fathers by Moses. And thou, that hast been the author of all mischief against the Hebrews, shalt not escape the hands of God." After watching all her sons tortured to death, the mother followed them to her death, for she too refused to eat the swine's flesh as Antiochus had commanded (2 Macc 7:1-42).

History will repeat itself. In fact, the events that occurred during the reign of Antiochus Epiphanes and brought on the Maccabean revolt will find a strange repetition during the Antichrist's reign in the latter part of the tribulation period. This is why Daniel views Antiochus as a type of the Antichrist, and for this same reason his description of Antiochus merges with a preview of the Antichrist (11:21 ff.). The transition from Antiochus to the Antichrist actually occurs at verse 36 in Daniel 11. As Antiochus desired to force Greek culture upon the Jews, so the Antichrist will try to force the cult of the beast, or the worship of himself, upon the Jews. However, unlike the adherents of the apostate church, the Jews will resist the Antichrist, just as their forefathers resisted Antiochus centuries before.

The persecution of Israel that Jesus predicts in His prophetic discourse (Mt 24:15-28), which follows in the three and one-half years after the breaking of the covenant and the cessation of the temple sacrifices, is also pictured in Revelation 12:1, "And a great sign was seen in heaven." The King James Version translates this as a "wonder." Living Letters suggests that a "pageant," depicting the dramatic conflict between Satan and Israel, is what is being viewed. The "pageant" character of what John views is mentioned twice (vv. 1, 3).

The conflict begins when the woman (Israel) gives birth to a child (the Lord Jesus Christ). The wrath of the great red dragon (Satan) is aimed at the child; however, since Israel is the host of the child in the world, the dragon's wrath is directed against Israel. The child escapes the injury of the dragon for he is caught up to the throne of God.

The great parenthesis occurs between verses 5 and 6. Then, after more than two thousand years, the conflict will contin-

ue in the great-tribulation period. The duration of the conflict is "a thousand two hundred and threescore days" (v.
6), that is, three and one-half years. This fact is restated in
verse 14 by the cryptic use of a "time" (one year), "times"
(two years), and a "half a time" (one-half year), totaling
three and one-half years.

It has been Satan's plan to destroy Israel and thus to frus-
trate God's purposes. That attempt will be intensified during the last part of the tribulation period: "And the serpent
cast out of his mouth after the woman water as a river, that
he might cause her to be carried away by the stream" (Rev
12:15). Since he cannot destroy Israel nationally nor touch
the 144,000, Satan finally concentrates upon those individuals in Israel who will accept Jesus as their Messiah during
the tribulation and before Israel (nationally) does so at the
close of the tribulation period: "And the dragon waxed wroth
with the woman, and went away to make war with the rest
of her seed, that keep the commandments of God, and hold
the testimony of Jesus" (v. 17). It is the wrath of Satan,
therefore, that is behind the martyrdom of these saints.

In considering the religious conditions during the last half
of the tribulation period, we must not only look at the destiny
of the apostate church which is destroyed, and the nation
Israel who suffers persecution and whose Levitical worship
is suppressed, but at two other groups that play a vital part
in the religious and spiritual character of the time. They are
the 144,000 and the two witnesses.

The 144,000 maintain essentially the same testimony during the great tribulation period that they did during the
first three and one-half years. They continue to preach the
kingdom of God and to offer the Lord Jesus Christ as Israel's Messiah and the Gentile's Saviour. Many, both Jews
and Gentiles, apparently respond to their message and are
saved. Those who respond also apparently suffer martyrdom,
though the 144,000 remain untouched during the entire pe-

riod. It is the martyr's chorus, the cry of those who have been saved and martyred during the tribulation period, that is heard repeatedly in the chapters of the Revelation that cover the tribulation period.

In addition to the above, there emerges during the great-tribulation period two strange figures who "shall prophesy a thousand two hundred and threescore days, clothed in sackcloth" (Rev 11:3). These 1,260 days equal three and one-half years. Therefore, their witness occurs during the last half of the seventieth week of Daniel.

Revelation 11 begins with a summons to John to measure the temple. Apparently something is about to happen in the temple, for in the Old Testament, things are often measured in view of destruction (see 2 Ki 21:13; Is 34:11; Amos 7:7-9). Though we cannot be certain why John is instructed to measure the temple, it may be that God is going to destroy it. This is also suggested by the fact that at the end of the three and one-half year witness of the two prophets, an earthquake destroys a tenth part of the city (Rev 11:13). The earthly temple is probably demolished in this cataclysm because, beginning with verse 19, only the heavenly sanctuary remains in view. Why is God about to destroy this temple, only so recently built and employed by Israel in a revival of the Levitical system? It must be destroyed because at midtribulation it will be desecrated beyond anything that has ever happened.

The temple in Jerusalem had been desecrated many times in ancient history. According to the Midrashic Rabbi Aha, when "the wicked Titus" entered the holy of holies in the temple he brought with him two Jewish harlots and, spreading out the scroll of the law on the altar, he ordered them to lie upon it. Titus then violated the sacred Scriptures. This symbolic profaning of the temple by Titus was continued by his armies who sexually abused the priests and the Levites. The holy place, while it stood, was turned into a house of prostitution where Jewish females and boys suffered at the hands of the Roman soldiers.

Antiochus desecrated the temple in his day by offering swine upon the altar. But when Antiochus Epiphanes profaned the temple in his day, it was recovered and cleansed three years later by Judas Maccabaeus (1 Macc 4:36 ff.). A new altar was made to Yahweh of freshly gathered unhewn stones and, in order that the altar fires be new and pure, priests rubbed flints together to get a newly created spark to ignite new altar fires. Old and desecrated vessels were replaced. A feast of rededication was held on the twenty-fifth day of the Hebrew month Kisleu, 164 b.c., and it was decreed that this day be kept for a memorial. The Jewish Feast of Lights (Hanukkah) celebrates to this day that recovery and dedication of the temple again to the Lord.

But this will not be the case in the future temple. When it is desecrated, only destruction is sufficient to erase the abomination of desolation which has violated its sacred precincts. Jesus in His prophetic discourse instructs those who witness the establishment of the abomination in the temple to flee the city of Jerusalem (Mt 24:15 ff.). One reason is that they will be persecuted if they do not worship the image of the beast, but a second cause for leaving is that the city will then be in danger of imminent destruction.

Jesus indicated three eventualities that would add to the crisis of those who flee (Mt 24:19-20): First, if they have an unweaned child to care for, or second, if their exit occurs in winter, these two things would obviously complicate their escape; and third, it would be difficult if they have to flee on the Sabbath (v. 20). Evidently the Levitical system, in force during the first three and one-half years of the period, has not yet had time to be abolished by the Antichrist, and this could limit their escape, at least morally, to a Sabbath day's journey which is only between 1,000 and 1,200 yards, or the distance from Jerusalem out to the Mount of Olives (Ac 1:12).

Obviously this would not carry them far enough away to escape.

The temple is desecrated by the placing of the abomination of desolation, the image of the beast, in it. Not only did Jesus refer to this in His prophetic discourse, but Paul also mentions it: "The man of sin [is to] be revealed, the son of perdition, he that opposeth and exalteth himself against all that is called God or that is worshipped; so that he sitteth in the temple of God, setting himself forth as God" (2 Th 2: 3-4). Daniel indicates that this will happen after the burnt offering is made to cease—when the Antichrist breaks the covenant with Israel in the midst of the week (Dan 12:11).

When this happens, some are to flee Jerusalem, Jesus said, but at the same time the two mysterious prophets will arrive in Jerusalem. They will prophesy in sackcloth, which speaks of impending disaster (Is 37:1 ff.; Dan 9:3). Revelation 11:4 identifies them with "two olive trees" and "two candlesticks." This brings to mind Zerubbabel and Joshua the high priest, in Zechariah 4 and 5, whose labors also had to do with the temple, for they appeared after the exile to inspire Judah to rebuild the fallen temple. They may be set in deliberate contrast to the two, for where Zerubbabel and Joshua spoke of rebuilding the temple, the two will speak of destroying the temple due to the presence of the abomination.

Like the 144,000, they are invincible until their work is finished (Rev 11:5). But, having completed their witness, they will be killed and their bodies will lie unburied in the streets of Jerusalem for three and one-half days. Jesus' body was laid in a tomb, and when He arose from the dead, many said that His body had been stolen by His disciples. But no one will doubt the resurrection of these two. They will then be raptured, for a voice will call them to heaven and they will go up in a cloud as the world looks on (v. 12). At that point the city is shaken by an earthquake (v. 13), and apparently the temple is destroyed, as the witnesses prophesied. This

advances the narrative to the close of the tribulation period
when the temple is destroyed. However, it must be remembered that with the introduction of each new character in
Revelation 11–13, the chronology returns each time to the
beginning of the great-tribulation period.

Who are these two witnesses? Are they identified in Scripture? One seems to be Elijah. The last verses in the Old
Testament promised that Elijah would return: "Behold, I
will send you Elijah the prophet before the great and terrible
day of Jehovah come. And he shall turn the heart of the
fathers to the children, and the heart of the children to
their fathers" (Mal 4:5-6; cf. 3:1-3). But was this prediction
not fulfilled in the ministry of John the Baptist? Did not
Jesus say, "And if ye are willing to receive it, this is Elijah,
that is to come"—speaking of John the Baptist (Mt 11:14)?

In a certain sense John the Baptist was a fulfillment of
this prediction. But Matthew 17:11-12, makes a dual reference to the fulfillment of Malachi's prediction: "Elijah indeed
cometh, and shall restore all things: but I say unto you, that
Elijah is *come* already, and they knew him not, but did unto
him whatsoever they would." Elijah "cometh." This is a future anticipation of the ministry of Elijah during the great
tribulation when he is used of God to prepare Israel for
their great restoration at Christ's second coming. But Jesus
also said, "Elijah is come." This is a reference to the immediate ministry of John the Baptist which ended, not in the
victory that Malachi predicted of Elijah's ministry, but in
the death of the prophet, as Jesus indicates.

But notice that even in Matthew 11:14 there is a conditional statement. Jesus said, "And *if* ye are willing to receive
it, this is Elijah, that is to come." Receive what? The "it"
is supplied for the word "receive" has no expressed object.
Does "it" refer to the Elijahlike character of John the Baptist
or to the kingdom of God? Jesus could be saying in effect:
"*If* you are willing to receive the kingdom of God, *then* John

the Baptist is Elijah." But they were not, and therefore Elijah must yet come in order to prepare Israel for the reception of the kingdom. This he will do during the great-tribulation period as he appears as one of the two witnesses. Some of the early church Fathers held the view that there would be two advents of Elijah, one in the spirit of John the Baptist, and the other literally at the time of the end.

It is interesting that the recently published *New Catholic Encyclopedia* devotes a full-column article to "Elia, Second Coming of." In this article on the future return of Elijah to the earth it poses this question :". . . is one to look for Elia himself to reappear in eschatological times," since John the Baptist obviously did not fulfill Malachi's prediction? Its answer is twofold. Though modern theologians tend to find Malachi's prediction about the return of Elijah spiritually fulfilled in John the Baptist, the early church Fathers expected a literal fulfillment. The clearest of these patristic views is found in St. Augustine. "As there are two comings of the Judge," he writes, "there will be two heralds. The Judge sent before him the first herald [John the Baptist] calling him Elia, because Elia would be in the Second Coming what John was in the first."[1]

St. Augustine in *The City of God* says that not only will Elijah return to earth in the last days, but he will be a mighty influence in turning the Jews to the Messiah.[2] Though Malachi suggests that this is the purpose in the second coming of Elijah, he does not say how Elijah will accomplish this. It is St. Augustine's suggestion that he will accomplish this by "explaining in a spiritual sense the law which the Jews now understand in a carnal sense." When the Jews understand the law in its spiritual sense, as Moses did for example, St. Augustine's thesis is that they will then realize that Jesus is the Messiah.

[1]Augustine, *In evang. Ioh*, 4:5.
[2]Augustine, *The City of God*, 20:29.

In passing, this idea *does* relieve the problem of coercion in the conversion of the Jews. Many have assumed that Jesus will force the Jews to believe and thus accept Him as Messiah when He comes again. However, this can hardly be the case. They *will* accept Him as Messiah in His second coming, but not because they are forced to do so. The Jews will be greatly influenced by the teaching of the two witnesses and, as a result of Elijah's ministry during the three and one-half years before the second coming, the Jews will be all but ready and anxious to receive Jesus, the real Messiah.

The other witness has been variously identified. Moses and Enoch are the two most often mentioned. Enoch is often suggested because he, like Elijah, did not experience death and will do so for the first time here in the tribulation. Moses has been suggested because of the similarity between the signs that the two witnesses perform and those that Moses performed while contending with Pharaoh before the exodus from Egypt. But, can Moses die twice? Lazarus did! Moses is the more likely candidate of the two because he appears in the context of the Elijah prophecy in Malachi 4:5 (cf. v. 4). He is also with Elijah on the mount of transfiguration, and both the enemies of Moses and Elijah in the Old Testament are destroyed just as they are in the Revelation (cf. Num 16: 35 and 2 Ki 1:9 ff.).

WHAT CHANGES THE ANTICHRIST?

The Antichrist arises early in the tribulation as head of the revived Roman Empire. Even with this extensive political dominion he still feels a need for the allegiance of Judaism and the world church. What is it that liberates him from the need of their support and enables him in the great tribulation to turn upon the very forces of religion that he used early in his career to support his cause? It may be an event described by the prophet Ezekiel in chapters 38 and 39.

In the last days when Israel has been gathered back to the land and is dwelling there safely and securely (Eze 38:8, 11, 14), she will be attacked by a foe named Gog from the land of Magog (38:2). This foe, which comes from the far north (38:5, 15; 39:2) and swarms down over Palestine (38:9), will be utterly and decisively defeated (38:17—39:20). These are the facts. Now, what is their meaning?

The foe seems to be some sort of northern confederacy. Their leader is called Gog and is identified as the Prince of Rosh (Eze 38:3). This name "Prince of Rosh" does not appear in the King James Version or in the Revised Standard Version. Rosh is often translated as a common noun meaning "head" or "chief." Hence, the "chief prince of Meshech and Tubal" (RSV). However, most interpreters understand it to be a proper noun and translate it as does the New English Bible, for example, "the prince of Rosh, Meshech, and Tubal." His land is called Magog and is probably composed of these three districts, Rosh, Meshech and Tubal. The great Hebrew lexicographer, Gesenius identifies these three names with Russia, Moscow and Tobolsk, respectively. Others, just as renowned as he (e. g., Brown-Driver-Briggs), have rejected this identification.

But, no matter who the foe might be, he comes from the far north. Many peoples are allied with him, including Persia, Cush, Put, Gomer and Togarmah (38:5-6, 15). However, this is not an exhaustive list of the allies of this Prince of Rosh. "Many people with thee" (38:6) suggests an extensive alliance of powers against Israel in the last days.

But there may be more. Daniel 11:40 states that the king of the south (Egypt?) also comes against Israel at the same time as does the northern confederation. Both will attack Israel, but since the Antichrist has made a covenant with Israel, this will involve the forces of the revived Roman Empire in Israel's defense. (The same situation exists in the Holy Land today, for the defense of Israel could plunge the

West into conflict with the Arabs and Russia at any time.)
The enemies will be beaten and Israel's benefactor, the Antichrist, will then be the most powerful dictator in the world.

He apparently does not permanently subdue the Orient,
however, for the kings from the sunrising (Rev 16:12) come
against him in Palestine toward the close of the tribulation
period. The invasion of these Oriental kings is the gloomy
tidings that the Antichrist hears from the east and the north
in Daniel 11:44. (All invasions of Palestine came either from
the north or the south in ancient times. The Mediterranean
Sea and the Arabian Desert prevented invasions from the
east or west directly into Palestine. Thus, the Oriental kings,
though they come from the east across the dried-up Euphrates River, must move around the fertile crescent and descend
from the north into Palestine.) However, this invasion by the
kings from the sunrising occurs at the close of the tribulation
period, for Daniel says that the Antichrist comes to an end
as a result of this conflict (11:45).

But what about the invasion of the northern confederation
along with the king of the south? When does it occur? The
fact that it happens at a time when Israel is at peace and
resting in security would suggest the only time possible,
namely, the first part of the tribulation when Israel is still
under the protection of the covenant made with the Antichrist. Therefore, this war in Palestine between the northern confederation (allied with the southern king) against the
revived Roman Empire (along with Israel), in which the
former is defeated, is the decisive event that places the Antichrist in a position of world power. Only the Orient seems
not to have been permanently subdued by the Antichrist.
He will contend with them at the close of the tribulation period. At midtribulation, however, having defeated the northern and southern opposition in Palestine, his position is un-
contested in that part of the world.

It is at midtribulation, when the Antichrist arrives at this position of strength, with all his immediate foes defeated, that he turns upon Israel, thus breaking the covenant in the midst of the years, as Daniel predicted.

The reason why he turns upon the nation Israel is twofold. First, it is because he wishes to be worshiped as god. Antiochus IV had "Epiphanes," which means "God made manifest," added to his name. He wanted all his subjects to to worship him as god. Many Jews in the second century B.C. fled Jerusalem to seek refuge in the countryside, or to Alexandria in Egypt where they would be safe under the tolerant rule of the Ptolemies. Therefore, just as many Jews resisted pagan worship in the days of Antiochus Epiphanes, so many in Israel will resist the worship of the beast. And just as this defiance in the second century B.C. invited the wrath of Antiochus against their forefathers, so will this later resistance invite the wrath of the beast against them.

But, second, behind the wrath of the beast is Satan, as Revelation 12 suggests. Satan knows that if he can get rid of Israel, God's purposes in the coming of the Messiah will be defeated. So for three and one-half years, Satan's wrath, manifest through the Antichrist and the false prophet, will be vent against Israel and, as Jesus predicted in His prophetic discourse, "then shall be great tribulation, such as hath not been from the beginning of the world until now, no, nor ever shall be. And except those days had been shortened, no flesh would have been saved: but for the elect's sake [Israel] those days shall be shortened" (Mt 24:21-22).

ANTICHRIST'S APPEAL AS A FALSE GOD

Jesus warns of false Christs and false prophets who will arise during the great-tribulation period. This is actually the third warning in His prophetic discourse about false Christs (cf. vv. 5, 11). Therefore, each of the three eras the time of *travail,* the time of *tribulation,* and the time of *great tribulation,* will see the rise of false Messiahs.

From the petty impostors of the first century to the final impostor of the great tribulation, as each period intensifies, these unholy deceivers will be more persuasive in their appeal, until finally the beast and the false prophet make their most convincing appeal for the Antichrist to be accepted in the place of Israel's real God. Many in Israel will refuse to worship the image of the beast and will suffer the intense persecution of which Jesus speaks in Matthew 24:21-22. However, others in Israel will yield to the beast, just as many in Israel yielded to the Hellenizing edicts of Antiochus Epiphanes.

How does the Antichrist make his appeal as a false God? Daniel (9:27; 12:11), Jesus (Mt 24:15), Paul (2 Th 2:4) and John (Rev 13:14) all speak of something that suggests an image or likeness of the beast that is placed in the temple. This image is given breath and made to speak (Rev 13:15). Those that do not worship it are killed.

The worship of the image is accomplished through the mediation of another figure called the false prophet who emerges in Revelation 13:11 ff. The false prophet is to the beast what Menelaus was to Antiochus Epiphanes.

The two together—the beast as an object of worship, and the false prophet as the inspiration of such worship—deceive many during this time. However, the dynamic which the false prophet lends to the worship of the beast cannot account entirely for the worship given him. The personality of the beast himself also inspires worship.

His military and political genius has already been demonstrated as he heads the revived Roman Empire and then at midtribulation when he becomes a virtual world dictator. But there must be a religious genius about him also. This is reminiscent of Augustus Caesar who ushered in the golden age of the Roman Empire and whom the Romans called a god. The Roman Senate officially deified Augustus after his death, and shrines to him were built throughout the empire.

The Antichrist also has this aura of deity about him, but he will be deified in his lifetime, as were some of the later Caesars.

In Zechariah 11 the prophet is called of God to act out the part of a shepherd. This shepherd is pictured by Zechariah as being rejected by Israel and finally sold for thirty pieces of silver (11:13), things which happened to Israel's Messiah when He came the first time and died upon the cross. It is interesting that Ezekiel predicts that Israel will finally accept this Shepherd (34:23). However, it is the prophet Zechariah who sees another fact, namely, before Israel accepts the true Shepherd as Messiah, they will first turn to a false shepherd. Zechariah calls him a "foolish shepherd" and a "worthless shepherd" (11:15, 17). This is the Antichrist whom many in Israel will accept as their long-awaited Messiah.

The chief passages in Scripture that deal with the personality, career and destiny of the Antichrist, in addition to Jesus' prophetic discourse in Matthew 24, are Daniel 7:7-8, 20-22; 8:23-25; 9:26-27; 11:36-45; 2 Thessalonians 2:1-10; Revelation 13:1-18; 17:8-14. Many aspects of his career cannot be considered within the scope of this work. However, since Jesus in His prophetic discourse warned of him as a spiritual deceiver, the nature of his relationship to the people of God may be seen in several of these Scripture passages.

The Antichrist appears in Revelation 13 in association with the false prophet. Since the Antichrist is also under Satan's motivating influences, this would suggest a diabolical trinity which is intended to counterfeit the divine Trinity (cf. Rev 16:13). Satan as opposed to God, the Antichrist as opposed to Jesus Christ, and the false prophet as opposed to the Holy Spirit, compose this false trinity of the tribulation.

This analogy in itself suggests that the Antichrist's chief end is to achieve the worship of man. This is also brought out by Paul: "he that opposeth and exalteth himself against all

that is called God or that is worshipped; so that he sitteth in
the temple of God, setting himself forth as God" (2 Th 2:4).

Daniel indicates this same thing in 11:35-37 when he
moves from a description of Antiochus Epiphanes to one of
the Antichrist, whom he calls "the king [that] shall do according to his will." The Antichrist is then characterized: "He
shall exalt himself, and magnify himself above every god,
and shall speak marvellous things against the God of gods;
and he shall prosper till the indignation be accomplished; for
that which is determined shall be done. Neither shall he regard the gods of his fathers ["Elohim" and not "Yahweh"],
nor the desire of women, nor regard any god; for he shall
magnify himself above all."

As a result of his place in the diabolical trinity, Satan gives
to him his "power, and his throne, and great authority" (Rev.
13:2). The false prophet gives the inspiration of worship to
the Antichrist, just as the Holy Spirit does to Jesus (Jn 16:
13-14), and just as the Benjaminite High Priest Menelaus did
to Antiochus Epiphanes (cf. Rev 13:12). But, in addition,
the Antichrist comes in his own name, whereas the Lord
Jesus came in the name of His Father: "I am come in my
Father's name, and ye receive me not: if another shall come
in his own name, him ye will receive" (Jn 5:43). Therefore,
the person and office of each member of the diabolical trinity
lends impetus to the worship of the Antichrist.

It is in the light of all that Scripture has to say about the
Antichrist and his deceptive program to achieve the worship
of men that Jesus' warning in Matthew 24 must be interpreted. The Lord Jesus ends His discussion of the great-
tribulation period by saying, "Behold, I have told you before-
hand. If therefore they shall say unto you, Behold he is in
the wilderness; go not forth: Behold he is in the inner cham-
bers; believe it not. For as the lightning cometh forth from
the east, and is seen even unto the west; so shall be the com-

ing of the Son of man. Wheresoever the carcase is, there will the eagles be gathered together" (24:25-28).

This statement suggests that when the Messiah does come at the end of the age, it will not be as the Antichrist will come. Christ's coming will be characterized by two things: first, with great observation (v. 27), and second, amid great carnage (v. 28). This brings us to the next phase of Jesus' discourse, namely, that of the times "after the tribulation" (vv. 29 ff.). This time is ushered in by the second coming of Christ and the Battle of Armageddon, that is, the great observation and great carnage of verses 27 and 28.

7

Immediately After the Tribulation

Matthew 24:29-34

IN VERSES 29-34 of His great prophetic discourse, Jesus presents three things that will occur next in the order of prophetic events concurrent with the close of the tribulation period: First, the Battle of Armageddon (v. 29), then the second coming of Christ (v. 30), and third, the final regathering of the nation Israel (v. 31). These three events wind up the tribulation period and conclude God's dealing with Israel in order to prepare the Jews for the coming of the Messiah. The Battle of Armageddon crushes the Antichrist's kingdom and rids the world of his dominion. With this false Messiah swept away, Jesus, the true Messiah, returns to the earth with great power and glory. It is then that unbelieving Israel, who has passed through the sorrow of the great-tribulation period, is regathered and she finally accepts Jesus as the long-anticipated Messiah.

THE BATTLE OF ARMAGEDDON

"But immediately after the tribulation of those days the sun shall be darkened, and the moon shall not give her light, and the stars shall fall from heaven, and the powers of the heavens shall be shaken" (Mt 24:29).

These are all celestial events that indicate a universal upheaval that immediately precedes Christ's second coming. With an earth-oriented perspective rather than a celestial one, as is in Jesus' prophetic discourse, Revelation 16 suggests similar catastrophic events when the first five bowls, containing the wrath of God, are poured out upon the earth. These five bowls immediately precede the sixth bowl containing the Battle of Armageddon (Rev 16:12-16).

Jesus' words suggest a celestial cataclysm. However, His words probably reflect the heavenly consequences of earth's greatest catastrophe, the Battle of Armageddon. So awesome and fierce is this final human convulsion upon the earth that it arises in a great crescendo of agony up to the celestial sphere, causing the sun to become dark, the moon not to give her light, the stars to fall, and the powers of the heavens to be shaken.

What is the nature of this earthly event that can have such cosmic consequences? Undoubtedly the full force of what Jesus says could not occur without this being a traumatic preparation for His second coming. Therefore, the Battle of Armageddon alone could not fully account for what Jesus sees in the celestial sphere. However, though this heavenly phenomena precedes the second coming, it is adjacent to the great earthly conflagration of Armageddon. Therefore, Jesus' words may describe a dramatic interlude that both precedes His second coming and succeeds the great battle.

The name Armageddon (Rev 16:16) may be derived from the Hebrew *Har-Megiddo,* which means "Mountain of Megiddo." Even this is unsure. Megiddo was an ancient Canaanite city located ten miles south of Nazareth and fifteen miles inland from the Mediterranean Sea in the Valley of Jezreel in Central Palestine. The Greeks called it the Plain of Esdraelon. This plain runs from Mount Carmel southeast across Palestine. The ancient city of Megiddo commanded a pass where a road cut through the Mount Carmel ridge leading from the coast—the Plain of Sharon—and ran into the Valley of Jezreel. Megiddo thus commanded the direct road from Egypt and the coast of Palestine into Galilee, Syria and Mesopotamia. It was the scene of some of the bloodiest battles of ancient history. Here Israel won a victory over Sisera and his host (Judg 5:19, cf. 4:1-16). The fatal struggle between King Josiah of Judah and Pharaoh Necoh also took place here (2 Ki 23:29; 2 Ch 35:22). And the final battle of modern history will take place here at the close of the tribulation.

Though the book of the Revelation locates the battle near the ancient city of Megiddo in the Plain of Jezreel (Hebrew) or Esdraelon (Greek), the prophet Joel locates the battle in the Valley of Jehoshaphat (3:2-17, especially vv. 2, 12). It is also called "the valley of decision" (v. 14). The location of the Valley of Jehoshaphat cannot now be identified. Though the name may be purely symbolic—the Hebrew means "God judges," later tradition, both Jewish and Christian, placed the location of the valley in the vicinity of Jerusalem, in the Kidron Valley between the temple hill and the Mount of Olives. Others have identified it with the "king's dale" where Absalom erected a pillar or funeral monument near which he expected to be buried (2 Sa 18:18). According to Josephus, the monument stood about four hundred yards north of Jerusalem. Both locations, then, would suggest that the final battle occurs in the immediate vicinity of the city of Jerusalem.

Both the prophet Zechariah (12:1-12; 14:1-4) and the prophet Micah (4:11-13) locate the battle in the city itself. Isaiah (34:1-7; 63:1-4) pictures the Lord coming up from Edom in the south of Palestine. Daniel (11:45) describes the Antichrist coming to his end in Palestine between the Mediterranean Sea and the glorious holy mountain, Jerusalem. Revelation 14:20 tells of blood running from sixteen hundred furlongs in the land, which is about the length of Palestine from north to south, a little less than two hundred miles.

All of this suggests that the final battle may not be limited to one spot in Israel. Rather, it may be fought over the entire area of the Holy Land. In Revelation 16:14 it is called "the war of the great day of God, the Almighty" (RV). Just as any war is made up of many battles, so history's final war may be composed of many battles that roam over the map of the Holy Land.

In addition to several locations for the final battle, or war of Armageddon, many expositors believe that the time of the war is not limited to just one event which terminates the tribulation. Rather, it comprehends all the battles that rage during the first part of the tribulation, beginning with the invasion of Palestine by the foe from the north (Eze 38–39) and running the entire three and one half-year period of the great tribulation, and climaxing with the war described by the prophets Joel, Zechariah, Micah and Isaiah, and by the outpouring of the sixth bowl in Revelation 16:12-16.

However, Revelation 16:12-16 seems to indicate that it is a specific invasion of Palestine that signals the Battle of Armageddon: "And the sixth poured out his bowl upon the great river, the river Euphrates; and the water thereof was dried up, that the way might be made ready for the kings that come from the sunrising" (v. 12). This suggests an invasion from the Orient. It might be the same invasion, the tidings of which trouble the Antichrist in Daniel: "But tidings out of the east and out of the north shall trouble him; and he shall go forth with great fury to destroy and utterly to sweep away many. And he shall plant the tents of his palace between the sea and the glorious holy mountain; yet he shall come to his end, and none shall help him" (11:44-45).

Apparently the Antichrist never completely subjects the Orient to his world empire, for near the close of the great-tribulation period its leaders are able to mount a rebellion against him and to influence others to join in this revolt (Rev 16:14). It is the tidings of this invasion from across the dried-up Euphrates River which the Antichrist hears and is troubled by. The tidings come from the east, but Daniel adds that they are from the north also. Since the Antichrist has already defeated the northern confederacy, this must mean that the Oriental invasion has followed the fertile crescent and is now descending upon Israel from the north.

As a result of this invasion and subsequent battle, the Antichrist "shall come to his end, and none shall help him" (Dan 11:45). Therefore, the times of the Gentiles close in this great battle which erupts in Palestine between the forces of the Antichrist and the Oriental hordes.

In the midst of this great conflagration a third force, the returning Lord Jesus Christ and His saints, intervenes: "And to these also Enoch, the seventh from Adam, prophesied, saying, Behold, the Lord came with ten thousands of his holy ones, to execute judgment upon all" (Jude 14-15; cf. Zec 14:5; Col 3:4).

As a result of this final world conflict, the Antichrist and his empire are defeated (Dan 11:45; Rev 16:10); the Antichrist and the false prophet are cast into the lake of fire (Rev 19:20; 20:10); and the devil is bound in the abyss for a thousand years (Rev 20:1-4).

THE SECOND COMING OF CHRIST

"And then shall appear the sign of the Son of man in heaven: and then shall all the tribes of the earth mourn, and they shall see the Son of man coming on the clouds of heaven with power and great glory" (Mt 24:30).

Christ's second coming is a significantly different event from the rapture of the church which occurs before the tribulation period begins. In the rapture, the Lord Jesus comes as a thief in the night to secretly snatch away His church from the earth. But in His second coming, "Behold, he cometh with the clouds; and every eye shall see him, and they that pierced him; and all the tribes of the earth shall mourn over him" (Rev 1:7). It is to this universally visible event that the two men in white made reference in Acts 1:11, "Ye men of Galilee, why stand ye looking into heaven? This

Jesus, who was received up from you into heaven, shall so come in like manner as ye beheld him going into heaven." However, it is John in Revelation who portrays most dramatically the glory and power of the second coming of Christ:

> And I saw the heaven opened; and behold, a white horse, and he that sat thereon called Faithful and True; and in righteousness he doth judge and make war. And his eyes are a flame of fire, and upon his head are many diadems; and he hath a name written which no one knoweth but he himself. And he is arrayed in a garment sprinkled with blood: and his name is called The Word of God. And the armies which are in heaven followed him upon white horses, clothed in fine linen, white and pure. And out of his mouth proceedeth a sharp sword, that with it he should smite the nations: and he shall rule them with a rod of iron: and he treadeth the winepress of the fierceness of the wrath of God, the Almighty. And he hath on his garment and on his thigh a name written, KING OF KINGS, AND LORD OF LORDS (Rev 19:11-16).

Just as the rapture has the church as its subject, so the second coming of Christ has the nation Israel as its subject. Though the second coming terminates the times of the Gentiles, and though the church comes with Christ in this advent, its primary reference is to the nation Israel. What results from the return of the Lord Jesus has almost exclusively to do with the nation Israel, for the church has already experienced resurrection and received her reward.

Since the second coming is primarily directed toward the nation Israel, it will have two significant emphases as far as Israel nationally is concerned. One is that the nation's spiritual conversion takes place in association with the second coming. The other is that a resurrection with Israel as its subject will occur at this time.

It is a mistake to conceive that at the rapture both the

Old Testament saints and the church are raised from the dead. The rapture is an exclusive church event and only the church is resurrected, as Paul clearly states: "For the Lord himself shall descend from heaven, with a shout, with the voice of the archangel, and with the trump of God: and *the dead in Christ* shall rise first; then we which are alive, that are left, shall together with them be caught up in the clouds, to meet the Lord in the air: and so shall we ever be with the Lord" (1 Th 4:16-17). Notice that only the dead "in Christ" are raised at the rapture. Those "in Christ" are a very special order in Paul's theology; they are the church, the body of Christ, a distinctive group. If this is the case, when are the Old Testament saints raised from the dead? The answer is: at Christ's second coming.

In Revelation 20:5 reference is made to "the first resurrection." In 1 Corinthians 15:23 Paul speaks of an order of resurrection events. Christ is "the firstfruits" in this order of resurrection. "Then they that are Christ's, at his coming." This indicates that the first resurrection is not one single event comprising one general resurrection of all the saved. Rather, the first resurrection is an *order* of resurrection events that is composed of several stages: first, the resurrection of Christ; second, the resurrection of the church as a distinctive group; third, the resurrection of both the Old Testament saints and the tribulation martyrs at the close of the tribulation period. It is this third group, namely, the Old Testament saints plus those who were saved and martyred during the tribulation period, who are raised from the dead at the second coming. For this reason Daniel speaks of a resurrection occurring after Israel's "time of trouble" (12:1-2).

FINAL REGATHERING OF THE NATION ISRAEL

"And he shall send forth his angels with a great sound of a trumpet, and they shall gather together his elect from the four winds, from one end of heaven to the other" (Mt 24:31).

These are Jesus' final words about events which bring to a close Israel's time of *travail, tribulation,* and *great tribulation.* The Lord's second coming ends the reign of the Antichrist and ushers in the reign of the Messiah. This golden age of Israel's Messianic era is pictured in hundreds of Old Testament passages. It is begun, Jesus says, by the gathering together of the elect, which occurs when Jesus comes again.

Israel is being regathered today. However, this is a regathering in unbelief. The people are coming back to the land in significant numbers and will probably continue to do so during much of the tribulation. Even today Israel is an independent state. But the regathering that occurs at the second coming is one that has Israel's spiritual regeneration in view as well as the nation's physical restoration.

God has never forgotten His covenant people during all these centuries of wandering among the Gentile nations: "And yet for all that, when they are in the land of their enemies, I will not reject them, neither will I abhor them, to destroy them utterly, and to break my covenant with them; for I am Jehovah their God; but I will for their sakes remember the covenant of their ancestors, whom I brought forth out of the land of Egypt in the sight of the nations, that I might be their God: I am Jehovah" (Lev 26:44-45). Israel will yet be remembered and returned to the land, a second time (Is 11:10-12).

This restoration was not fulfilled when Judah returned from Babylon in the fifth century b.c., for both Jeremiah and Amos suggest that Israel's final regathering will be permanent. They will never suffer expulsion from their homeland again: "For I will set mine eyes upon them for good, and I will bring them again to this land: and I will build them, and not pull them down; and I will plant them, and not pluck them up. And I will give them a heart to know me, that I am Jehovah: and they shall be my people, and I will be their God; for they shall return unto me with their whole heart"

(Jer 24:6-7). "And I will plant them upon their land, and they shall no more be plucked up out of their land which I have given them, saith Jehovah thy God" (Amos 9:15). Not by the wildest imagination can it be said that these two passages were fulfilled in the return from the Babylonian exile. They await a future fulfillment in association with Christ's second coming (cf. Ac 3:19-21; Eze 34:11-13).

However, more than physical restoration is promised. In each of these passages the physical restoration to the land is accompanied by a promise of spiritual regeneration. Therefore, when the Messiah comes, He will not only gather all His elect physically back to the land, many of whom are already there now, but in this regathering is the promise of renewed spiritual experience. It is then that Israel will yield to Jesus as Messiah, and the spiritual consequences which the prophets foresaw will be fulfilled.

In this regathering at His second coming, Israel will mourn over her sins: "And I will pour upon the house of David, and upon the inhabitants of Jerusalem, the spirit of grace and of supplication; and they shall look unto me [some mss. read 'him'] whom they have pierced; and they shall mourn for him, as one mourneth for his only son, and shall be in bitterness for him, as one that is in bitterness for his first-born. In that day shall there be a great mourning in Jerusalem" (Zec 12:10-11).

Israel will then be cleansed: "In that day there shall be a fountain opened to the house of David and to the inhabitants of Jerusalem, for sin and for uncleanness" (Zec 13:1). "But Judah shall abide for ever, and Jerusalem from generation to generation. And I will cleanse their blood [i.e., hold as innocent], that I have not cleansed: for Jehovah dwelleth in Zion" (Joel 3:20).

It is then that Israel will accept Jesus as her Messiah. Then shall be fulfilled the words of Jesus, uttered while He was leaving the temple to go out to the Mount of Olives where

He delivered His prophetic discourse: "Ye shall not see me henceforth, till ye shall say, Blessed is he that cometh in the name of the Lord" (Mt 23:30).

Israel will be spiritually reborn. It is interesting that the word "regeneration" is used only twice in the New Testament. It is used once for personal regeneration (Titus 3:5). The only other time, it is used in reference to the nation Israel: "And Jesus said unto them, Verily I say unto you, that ye who have followed me, in the regeneration when the Son of man shall sit on the throne of his glory, ye also shall sit upon twelve thrones, judging the twelve tribes of Israel" (Mt 19:28). Here the Lord promises His disciples a place of authority over Israel, but the point we need to see is that Jesus also promises Israel a national destiny—one of regeneration. This can only find fulfillment at His second coming, for it certainly was not fulfilled in His first coming, nor can it be spiritualized and applied in some vague way to the church.

A number of promises appear in the Old Testament which are unconditional in their affirmation that the Lord will deal spiritually with Israel in the last days after the people are regathered. And it is in *that precise order* that the promises appear: *regathering first, then spiritual renewal.*

> And Jehovah thy God will bring thee into the land which thy fathers possessed, and thou shalt possess it; and he will do thee good, and multiply thee above thy fathers. And Jehovah thy God will circumcise thy heart, and the heart of thy seed, to love Jehovah thy God with all thy heart, and with all thy soul, that thou mayest live (Deu 30:5-6).
>
> I will gather you from the peoples, and assemble you out of the countries where ye have been scattered, and I will give you the land of Israel. . . . And I will give them one heart, and I will put a new spirit within you; and I will take the stony heart out of their flesh, and will give them a heart

of flesh; that they may walk in my statutes, and keep mine
ordinances, and do them (Eze 11:17-20).

For I will take you from among the nations, and gather
you out of all the countries, and will bring you into your
own land. And I will sprinkle clean water upon you, and ye
shall be clean: from all your filthiness, and from all your
idols, will I cleanse you. A new heart also will I give you,
and a new spirit will I put within you; and I will take away
the stony heart out of your flesh, and I will give you a heart
of flesh (Eze 36:24-26).

In each of these passages the nation is first regathered. Spiritual renewal does not come until after they are back in the
land.

It is then that the new covenant will be fulfilled in Israel:

Behold, the days come, saith Jehovah, that I will make a
new covenant with the house of Israel, and with the house
of Judah: not according to the covenant that I made with
their fathers in the day that I took them by the hand to bring
them out of the land of Egypt; which my covenant they
brake, although I was a husband unto them, saith Jehovah.
But this is the covenant that I will make with the house of
Israel after those days, saith Jehovah: I will put my law in
their inward parts, and in their heart will I write it; and I
will be their God, and they shall be my people. And they
shall teach no more every man his neighbor, and every man
his brother, saying, Know Jehovah; for they shall all know
me, from the least of them unto the greatest of them, saith
Jehovah: for I will forgive their iniquity, and their sin will
I remember no more (Jer 31:31-34).

Since regeneration *is* experienced by the individual believer who constitutes the church in this age, the essence of
the new covenant *does* find fulfillment in the church (Heb
10:16 ff.). However, the literal fulfillment of Jeremiah's prediction of the new covenant is found in the nation Israel at
Christ's second coming. Jeremiah sets forth this fact in the

most concise of terms when he declares that the continuance
of Israel as a nation toward this final spiritual destiny is as
sure as is the light of the sun by day, and the moon and stars
by night, and the stirring up of the sea so that its waves roar
(31:35-36).

It is then that the Spirit will be poured out upon Israel:

> And I will put my Spirit within you, and cause you to
> walk in my statutes, and ye shall keep mine ordinances, and
> do them (Eze 36:27).
>
> And I will put my Spirit in you, and ye shall live, and I
> will place you in your own land: and ye shall know that I,
> Jehovah, have spoken it and performed it, saith Jehovah
> (Eze 37:14).
>
> And they shall know that I am Jehovah their God, in that
> I caused them to go into captivity among the nations, and
> have gathered them unto their own land; and I will leave
> none of them any more there; neither will I hide my face
> any more from them; for I have poured out my Spirit upon
> the house of Israel, saith the Lord Jehovah (Eze 39:28-29;
> cf. Is 32:13-15; 44:1-5).

Notice that all the spiritual blessings that God has promised the nation Israel are made in connection with the land.
They will not be fulfilled outside the land. But they will find
a literal fulfillment when Israel is back in the land again.

"WHEN SHALL THESE THINGS BE?"

The two questions of the disciples initiated Jesus' great
prophetic discourse on the Mount of Olives. First they had
asked, "When shall these things be?" (Mt 24:3). The "these
things" referred to the three things that Jesus had just stated
about Israel: first, the desolation of Israel's house (Mt 23:38);
second, the time when Israel would say, "Blessed is he that
cometh in the name of the Lord" (23:39); and third, the
destruction of the temple (24:1-2). All three of these events
comprise the content of "these things" in the disciple's ques-

tion. It is the answer to the question, "When shall these things be?" that Jesus sets forth in Matthew 24:4-31.

His answer may be summarized thus: "These things shall be after Israel's time of *travail* (vv. 4-8); and after Israel's time of *tribulation* (vv. 9-14); and after the time of Israel's *great tribulation* (vv. 15-28)." Though the destruction of the temple occurred in the time of Israel's travail, and the desolation of Israel's house occurred during the great parenthesis, between the time of *travail* and *tribulation,* the time when Israel will say, "Blessed is he that cometh in the name of the Lord" will not come until Christ's second coming "after the tribulation of those days," as Jesus develops it in verses 29-31.

The second question is answered in Matthew 24:32-33. The question was, "What shall be the sign of thy coming?" Jesus' answer: "Now from the fig tree learn her parable: when her branch is now become tender, and putteth forth its leaves, ye know that the summer is nigh; even so ye also, when ye see all these things, know ye that he is nigh, even at the doors."

When "all these things" are fulfilled, this is the sign for the coming of the son of man. The fulfillment of *some* of these things is not enough. It is the combination of *all* being fulfilled that is significant and constitutes the sign for His second coming. When the combination of "all these things" is seen, in other words, the completion of Israel's time of *travail, tribulation,* and *great tribulation,* then you can expect the return of the Lord Jesus.

It is so certain that the second coming will occur at this time that Jesus said, "This generation shall not pass away, till all these things be accomplished." What generation? The one He was addressing—His contemporaries—in that day? No. The generation meant is the one which will be alive when the culmination of "all these things" comes to pass. In *that* generation Jesus will come again.

This gives a clear date for His second coming: It will occur at the close of the great-tribulation period. In fact, the time of the second coming is never in doubt. It is the time of the rapture that is uncertain and for which we can set no date. But when the rapture does occur, then Christ's second coming will occur seven years later. Only the rapture is imminent; the second coming is not. It can only occur after the great-tribulation signs are fulfilled.

8

The Future and the Church

Matthew 24:35—25:30

THE PRIMARY THRUST of Jesus' great prophetic discourse is toward the nation Israel. However, His disciples were not only members of the nation Israel; they were soon to become members of the church, for at Pentecost the Holy Spirit would come and baptize all of them into the body of Christ. Then, in each new generation, when a person repents and believes the gospel, the Spirit of God will also unite that person to the body which is the church. Hence, the church will be in the process of formation from its beginning at Pentecost until it is completed and taken out of the world at the rapture.

Israel's destiny has been set forth in Jesus' discourse. Now, what is the relationship of the church to all these events? Does the great parenthesis isolate the church to a unique destiny with no concern for the prophetic events to be wrought out in Israel? Though the church, the body of Christ, will not go through the tribulation period when it runs its course upon earth, she has a designated responsibility in view of these coming events in Israel. This responsibility of the church is twofold: to *watch* and to *occupy* until the Lord returns. Jesus sets this forth in Matthew 24:35—25:30.

SIGNS OF THE RAPTURE

A marked change in Jesus' teaching method occurs at this point in His discourse, beginning at verse 35. In all the previous sections while addressing Israel, He used the clearest of terminology. Now, as He addresses the church, His method changes and He speaks almost exclusively in metaphor and parable in this section. But not only does His teaching method change; His style of teaching also shifts. Where, in addressing Israel, He spoke in terms of events that were sure and certain, for He was speaking of specific and identifiable times in Israel's national history, both past and future; now in addressing the church, He speaks in terms of events whose time is uncertain. Therefore, the combination of uncertainty and preparedness marks His teaching style in this section.

However, before setting forth the uncertain time of the rapture, He declares the unalterable fact that though we cannot be certain about the time of the rapture, the event itself is certain in the counsel of God, for, "Heaven and earth shall pass away, but my words shall not pass away" (Mt 24:35).

The *fact* of the rapture is certain; the *time* of the rapture is uncertain. But are there no signs that might indicate the nearing of the rapture? Yes, and they are of two kinds.

First, there are those signs that point toward Christ's second coming which will be fulfilled during the tribulation period. But if the church is taken out at the rapture before the tribulation begins, how can these signs be of significance to the church? Though these signs will be fulfilled during the tribulation period, certain world conditions must adjust themselves for the rapid fulfillment of these events during the limits of the tribulation period. This adjustment of events must occur before the tribulation has begun, hence they must also occur before the rapture. If they point forward to the nearing of the tribulation period with its climax in Christ's second coming, how much closer must be the rapture, seeing that it must occur before the tribulation period can begin.

Certain contemporary events may suggest the nearness of the tribulation, for they imply conditions that must prevail before the events of the tribulation can occur. One is the conditions in Europe which indicate a union of European countries into a United States of Europe, such as the Common Market. These conditions could set the stage for a rapid revival of the ancient Roman Empire among these United States of Europe, especially since most of them are within the boundary of the ancient Roman Empire. NATO could also indicate a move in this direction.

The rising strength of Red China indicates that there is substance to the prediction that the invasion of a great Oriental power will signal the Battle of Armageddon. Again, the strategic place of Russia in Middle East affairs is one of the most significant signs of our day. Russia is already allied with the Arabs against Israel. If Russia is Magog—and this is not to be dogmatic about the identification—then the invasion of Palestine described in Ezekiel 38 and 39 could happen at any time. Again, the tendency to one world government is more evident in our day than ever before in modern history. In fact, only two main forms of government prevail in the world today, represented by East and West: communism and democracy. Only the mythical "iron curtain" separates them. The balance of power could shift at any time toward the complete dominion of totalitarianism.

But the most significant event to occur in the twentieth century, which might indicate the preparation of events to usher in the tribulation period, is the new State of Israel. No other sign is more significant. In fact Jesus said it is *the* sign that will indicate the end of the age, for Israel is the budding fig tree. Though the Jews have been slowly filtering back to the land for the last half century, not until 1948 was the new State of Israel created by the United Nations. This, plus the 1967 Israeli-Arab war, which gave Israel clear control of Jerusalem and, for the time, eliminated the city of Gentile dominion, is the most important of current events that indicates the nearness of the time of Jacob's trouble, the tribulation period.

Since these events seem to be setting the stage for the tribulation events that we have enumerated, and since the return of the Lord for His church must precede the tribulation, this could indicate the nearness of the end of the age. However, in considering these world events we must remember that the Bible warns against the fallacy of setting dates for the Lord's return. This fallacy has been sustained in history as time has proven many a date-setter to be wrong.

We have only trends with which to deal—trends which might indicate to us today that the end of the age is near. However, these trends could radically change tomorrow and be emptied of all their prophetic significance. Nevertheless, as long as world conditions continue as they are, and even intensify in the direction in which they are now going, these may very well indicate the closing days of the church age.

In addition to these signs that must be fulfilled in the tribulation and which point forward to Christ's second coming, signs of another general type point forward to the church's rapture. They are the clear statements of Scripture about spiritual conditions at the close of the church age.

Interestingly enough, it is the later epistles of the New Testament, those written in the last few decades of the first century, that tell of conditions that will prevail during the last days. The church age will close, they say, in apostasy. The professing church will be marked by defection from orthodoxy, with its corresponding decline in faith and morals.

> But the Spirit saith expressly, that in later times some shall fall away from the faith, giving heed to seducing spirits and doctrines of demons, through the hypocrisy of men that speak lies, branded in their own conscience as with a hot iron; forbidding to marry, and commanding to abstain from meats, which God created to be received with thanksgiving by them that believe and know the truth (1 Ti 4:1-3).

But know this, that in the last days grievous times shall come. For men shall be lovers of self, lovers of money, boastful, haughty, railers, disobedient to parents, unthankful, unholy, without natural affection, implacable, slanderers, without self-control, fierce, no lovers of good, traitors, headstrong, puffed up, lovers of pleasure rather than lovers of God; holding a form of godliness, but having denied the power thereof: from these also turn away (2 Ti 3:1-5).

. . . knowing this first, that in the last days mockers shall come with mockery, walking after their own lusts, and saying, Where is the promise of his coming? For, from the day that the fathers fell asleep, all things continue as they were from the beginning of the creation. For this they wilfully forget, that there were heavens from of old, and an earth compacted out of water and amidst water, by the word of God; by which means the world that then was, being overflowed with water, perished (2 Pe 3:3-6).

Without exception, when the New Testament views the last days of this age, it views them with pessimism. Just before the Lord Jesus returns for His true church, the professing church will be characterized by a wholesale defection from the faith of the Bible. The world will not be won by the gospel. Laodicea and not Philadelphia will be the prevailing tendency of the time. It is in the midst of these days, marked by a lukewarm interest in churchism but devoid of any personal commitment to Jesus Christ, that the Lord will return for His own. When the true church is taken out at the rapture, the professing church will continue into the tribulation to form the great apostate world church.

Though these two areas may shed light upon the conditions that prevail in the closing days of the church age, and though the rapture is imminent as opposed to the second coming that can occur only after the tribulation, we must remember Jesus' words regarding this: "But of that day and hour knoweth no one, not even the angels of heaven, neither the Son, but the Father only" (Mt 24:36).

The Church's Responsibilities

The time of the rapture is imminent, but its time is also uncertain. In light of this, two things are incumbent upon the church. The church is to *watch* (Mt 24:37-44), and it is to *occupy* until Jesus comes (Mt 24:45–25:30). Watchfulness and faithfulness are the two things Jesus stresses in the remaining part of His prophetic discourse that pertains to the church. In this discourse the nation Israel has been confronted with many factual *events* concerning her destiny that will be wrought in history, but the church is presented with *attitudes*—attitudes that should obtain as she awaits the Lord's coming.

The first attitude that should characterize the church as this age runs its course is that of watchfulness (vv. 37-44). "Watch therefore: for ye know not on what day your Lord cometh" (v. 42). Watchfulness is necessary because the Lord's return will be sudden: "And as were the days of Noah, so shall be the coming of the Son of man" (v. 37). Noah had preached the coming destruction; however, none listened. Then suddenly, as his contemporaries were occupied in worldly pursuits, the flood came and took them all away; "so shall be the coming of the Son of man."

Even with Noah's preaching, his contemporaries were unprepared when the flood suddenly came. But this must not be true of the church, Jesus says. She must take seriously the truth of the Lord's imminent return and be watching for its sudden occurrence. Incidentally, the admonition to watchfulness would be nonsense if the Lord's return could not occur immediately. If any stated event, such as the church going through the tribulation period, were necessary, then it would be meaningless to urge watchfulness, as Jesus does here.

The Lord's return for the church is not only sudden, but it is also selective. Not all will be taken; a division will occur: "Then shall two men be in the field; one is taken, and one is left: two women shall be grinding at the mill; one is taken, and one is left" (Mt 24:40-41). This does not mean that some believers will be left, as a partial-rapture theory maintains. If only a group of the spiritually elite were taken, this would reflect upon the doctrine of justification and the sufficiency of Christ's finished work on the cross. Since all believers are declared perfectly righteous in the justifying work of Christ, there are none of inferior spiritual status who might be left when He comes for the church. All are justified; all will be taken. The division, rather than being between two levels of believers, the spiritual and carnal, is between saved and lost. The saved will be taken; the lost will be left. Jesus would admonish His hearers to make sure that they are among those who are in the body of Christ.

However, in admonishing the church to be watchful, in the rest of this section He also cautions her to be occupied until He comes (Mt 24:45-25:30). The wise servant is the one who does not dissipate his responsibility, but who is faithful until the Lord returns.

The church at Thessalonica was presented with the prophetic word by the apostle Paul perhaps more than any other church to which he ministered. However, many reacted in just the way that Jesus warns against here. They believed in Christ's imminent return and were watching for it, but they were not occupied while they watched. Many had quit their work and were sitting idly by awaiting the rapture of the church (2 Th 3:10-11).

Three parables in this section underscore the necessity of faithful service in the light of the church's imminent rapture: first, the parable of the faithful and evil servant (24:45-51); second, the famous parable of the ten virgins (25:1-13); third, the parable of the talents (25:14-30). Their meaning is obvious. But the fact that Jesus presented this truth in three different parables is significant. He sees the lack of faithful service until He comes again as the most serious threat to the church. Enamored by the truth of the Lord's soon return, the church in every age could be tempted to see herself in a unique position and thus to drift, assuming that Christ's return will occur momentarily. But her expectancy of the rapture in any given era of church history should never make her neglectful of her aggressive witness to the world. She is to be faithful in her witness until the very moment the trumpet sounds, announcing the meeting in the air.

9

The Future and the Gentile Nations

Matthew 25:31-46

HAVING SPOKEN to the nation Israel and to the church, Jesus now turns to the third group which has an important place in the prophetic Scriptures—the Gentile nations.

The times of the Gentiles have run their course, beginning with the Babylonian conquest of Judah in the sixth century B.C. and ending with the Battle of Armageddon at the close of the great tribulation. During the entire times of the Gentiles, the Jews have been at the mercy of the Gentile nations. The Gentiles have consistently mistreated the Jew by discriminating against him, by persecuting him, and finally by murdering him in mass executions. The Gentile nations have conspired against the Jew to completely annihilate him—all with apparent impunity. However, it is at the judgment of the nations which takes place after Christ's second coming that the issue of Gentile treatment of the Jew will be redressed.

God's program for the church ends in judgment—the judgment seat of Christ which occurs at the rapture and in which the believer will receive his rewards (Rev 22:12). God's program for the nation Israel ends in judgment—the judgment of the great tribulation in which Israel is prepared to accept her Messiah (Eze 20:33-39). Just so, God's program for the Gentile nations ends in judgment. This judgment is previewed in Matthew 25:31-46 and is probably the most misunderstood and the most misapplied portion of Scripture in

140

all the Bible. Though its principles may be spiritualized and applied to conditions and to people in any day, its precise application is to the Gentile nations and its precise issue is their treatment of the Jew.

First, the time of this judgment is clearly indicated: "But when the ·Son of man shall come in his glory, and all the angels with him, then shall he sit on the throne of his glory" (25:31). It is not the rapture, for the rapture is a secret coming in which the Lord comes as a thief in the night to steal away His church (cf. 24:43). This judgment occurs in association with Christ's second coming in great power and glory in which He mounts the throne to assume the reign of authority in the forthcoming millennial earth. This marks the event as one which occurs at the close of the tribulation period. It is also in association with the Battle of Armageddon, for the prophet Joel says, "For, behold, in those days, and in that time, when I shall bring back the captivity of Judah and Jerusalem, I will gather all nations, and will bring them down into the valley of Jehoshaphat; and I will execute judgment upon them there for my people and for my heritage Israel, whom they have scattered among the nations: and they have parted my land" (3:1-2).

Jesus told His disciples that they would sit upon twelve thrones and judge the twelve tribes of Israel (Mt 19:28). Just as the original disciples will judge Israel, it could be that the church will be associated with Christ in this judgment of the nations. When the apostle Paul wrote to the church at Corinth, censuring them for going to court with one another and standing trial before worldly judges, he indicated that the church was competent to judge in these earthly matters for they would be given the responsibility to judge in eternal matters: "Dare any of you, having a matter against his neighbor, go to the law before the unrighteous, and not before the saints? Or know ye not that the saints shall judge the world? And if the world is judged by you, are ye unworthy to judge the smallest matters? Know ye not that we shall judge angels? How much more, things that pertain to this life?" (1 Co 6:1-3).

The judgment of the angels can only be that judgment in which the fallen angels are judged and sentenced to the lake of fire, which, Jesus says here, was prepared for the devil and His angels (Mt 25:41). But what about the saints judging the world? When will this take place? Perhaps the answer is that the church is associated with Christ in this judgment of the nations. The fact that the church returns with Jesus in His glorious second coming would also confirm this association. But whether the church is active in this judgment or not, at least the time is clear. It occurs at Christ's second coming.

Second, who are the subjects of this judgment? The terms of this judgment have been misapplied to both the individual saints and sinners alike with little reference to the fact that Jesus indicates exactly who is the subject of this judgment: "And before him shall be gathered *all the nations*" (25:32). Individuals are not in view here, except as individuals make up nations. The judgment is concerning the *nations*. It is a moot question as to whether this is restricted to just those nations who dealt with the Jews, for good or for ill, during the tribulation period, or whether all the nations which have had anything to do with Jewish persecution during the entire period known as the times of the Gentiles are in view. The latter view would infer some sort of resurrection, which is not stated. But perhaps the lament of every Jew who has suffered persecution at the hands of the Gentile nations during the last twenty-five hundred years, since Nebuchadnezzar took Jerusalem in 587 B.C., *is* redressed here in this judgment. Though the centuries of Jewish grievances against Gentile mistreatment may come to focus here, nevertheless, the actual subjects of this judgment are probably those nations which survive the tribulation. The term "natoins" (*ethne*) is a common one which is frequently found in the Scriptures in reference to the non-Jewish races. The "nations" stand in contrast to "my brethren" (v. 40), which are the Jews and therefore Jesus' kinsmen according to the flesh.

The issue of the judgment seems, at first reading, to indicate that these will be saved or lost, blessed or cursed, because of their works. However, it has already been established that the gospel of the kingdom which will be preached during the tribulation will be a message of repentance and of the cleansing blood of the Lamb. Therefore, those who are saved in the tribulation period are saved on the basis of individual response.

Works in the tribulation period, as in this present age of grace, do not *merit* salvation; they *prove* salvation. These Gentiles are not saved because they treat the brethren (i.e., the Jews) kindly. They are kind to them because they are saved. Therefore, the essence of the judgment is the character of those who compose the nations. Their works are at issue because works reveal character, and their works during the tribulation period—especially their attitude toward the Jew—manifest their true character.

For this reason Jesus said, "I was hungry, and ye gave me to eat; I was thirsty, and ye gave me drink; I was a stranger, and ye took me in; naked, and ye clothed me; I was sick, and ye visited me; I was in prison, and ye came unto me" (Mt 25:35-36). When did they do all this? It was their attitude toward the Jew during the tribulation period. These were their works that revealed their true character. Because of their transformed character, and because their good works, especially their treatment of "my brethren" the Jews, prove their transformed character, they are to receive the kingdom prepared for them (v. 34), just as every other transformed individual will receive his part in the kingdom.

If some are already redeemed people before they stand

in the judgment, what is the purpose of this judgment? The judgments of God in Scripture do not determine destiny, for that is determined before one comes to judgment. In the judgment of the church associated with the rapture, for example, the issue of salvation is settled long before the believer stands before the judgment seat of Christ. He is there to make manifest his works and thus his reward.

The great white throne judgment (Rev 20:11 ff.) does not determine whether one is saved or lost. That issue was settled in this life. The purpose of that judgment is to determine, not if one will go to hell, but to make manifest the reason why he is going to hell.

So it is in the judgment of the nations. Whether the individuals who compose the nations are saved or lost is settled during the tribulation period. If they repented and were cleansed by the blood of the Lamb they would have already given evidence of this by their attitude toward the Jew. This is the point, for this is the tribulation *test* of salvation. During this age of grace, Paul makes the presence of the Holy Spirit (Ac 19:2) the test of salvation. John also makes righteousness the test of salvation (1 Jn 2:29). So the test of true religion during the tribulation period is somehow bound up with one's attitude toward the Jew.

What then is the issue of this judgment? It is to separate the sheep from the goats. Whether one is a sheep or a goat is settled before he gets to judgment. It is the public manifestation of this character that is the purpose of this judgment. These have looked kindly upon the plight of the suffering Jew during the tribulation period. The nature of their deeds of kindness toward the Jew, who suffers so intensely under the heel of the Antichrist, is suggested by Jesus:

> For I was hungry, and ye gave me to eat; I was thirsty, and ye gave me drink; I was a stranger, and ye took me in; naked, and ye clothed me; I was sick, and ye visited me; I was in prison, and ye came unto me. Then shall the right-

eous answer him, saying, Lord, when saw we thee hungry, and fed thee? Or athirst, and gave thee drink? And when saw we thee a stranger, and took thee in? Or naked, and clothed thee? And when saw we thee sick, or in prison, and came unto thee? (Mt 25:35-39).

The Lord now acknowledges that the stipulations of the covenant with Abraham are as valid at the end of God's program for Israel as they were at the beginning. This is the real point and the *key* to the judgment of the Gentile nations. The reward that the sheep and the goats receive is defined in terms of blessings and curses.

The use of these two words by Jesus bring us back to the Abrahamic covenant. He says to the sheep, "Come ye *blessed* of my Father" (v. 34); and to the goats, "Depart from me, ye *cursed*" (v. 41). Now read again the terms of the covenant with Abraham: "I will make of thee a great nation, and I will make thy name great; and be thou a blessing: and I will *bless* them that *bless* thee, and him that *curseth* thee will I *curse*: and in thee shall all the families of the earth be blessed" (Gen 12:2-3). Here in the final judgment of the Gentile nations, God's promise to Abraham is made manifest. So the real and underlying issue may be one of God's faithfulness to the Jew in keeping the terms of the covenant made so many centuries ago.

The nations' treatment of the Jew is important as an evidence of salvation, but here in this judgment it may be incidental to the great truth that the Lord tends to demonstrate, namely, His faithfulness to Israel in keeping the original terms of the Abrahamic covenant.

In their attitude toward Israel during the tribulation, the redeemed from among the Gentile nations have actually proved the validity of their salvation. However, in this attitude toward Israel they have gained the benefits promised in the ancient covenant made with Abraham. In addition, as they have treated Israel, so they have treated the Lord Jesus, for He says, "Verily I say unto you, Inasmuch as ye did it unto one of these my brethren, even these least, ye did it unto me" (Mt 25:40).

Here is the lesson that Antiochus Epiphanes never learned. He persecuted the Jews of his day and met his demise under the curse of God—whether he ever realized it or not.

Here is the lesson that Hitler never learned. He tried to exterminate the Jew. Today his body rots in an unmarked grave. He died under the curse of God just as surely as did Antiochus in the long ago—whether he ever realized that it was his treatment of the Jew that spelled his ultimate doom, or not.

Here is the lesson that the Antichrist will not learn during the tribulation period. He will severely persecute the nation Israel, but it will be in this persecution that he will bring God's ancient curse down upon his empire. And he shall come to his end struggling to put down the people of God who cannot be finally defeated because of the ancient covenant that will be as valid in the last days of Israel's history as it was in the first.

Arabs, supported by the Russians, struggle against Israel today. However, they will no more succeed in their violation of the sacred nation than did Israel's former foes, for God has declared unalterably and unequivocally: "I will bless them that bless thee, and him that curseth thee will I curse!"

10
Why Israel?

IN CONCLUSION it is important to notice that in the prophetic discourse Jesus weaves the destiny of the church and the nations around the destiny of the nation Israel. Israel is the hub of all the prophetic Word. If one understands the unalterable destiny of Israel in God's prophetic program, then one is rightly oriented to understand the prophetic program for the church and the Gentile nations. But if Israel's destiny is spiritualized then the related prophetic destiny of the church and the nations becomes inexact, indistinct and vapid.

For this reason amillennialism has no clearly defined program for the last days which seriously attempts to take into account the wealth of prophetic detail found in Scripture. Conservative amillennialism sees this age coming to a close in Christ's second coming, a general resurrection, and a general judgment which ushers both saved and lost into separate eternal abodes. In this thesis the windup of all history is immediate and concise. However, though there may be some appeal in the very simplicity of these few master strokes which spell the end of time, it does not do justice to the complex fabric of the prophetic Word.

One of the most appealing facets of the literal-futuristic interpretation of Bible prophecy is the sense of *completeness*. It seriously attempts to fit all that the Bible reveals into a coherent eschatological program. Moreover, this approach gives rise to a sense of *fitness* because the prophetic details *do* fit into a coherent scheme of future events. That

147

they do *fit* is a studied statement. It does not mean that they are *forced*—a priori—into a coherent scheme, as some critics would infer.

However, though the literal-futuristic interpretation of Bible prophecy commends itself because of its comprehensive inclusion of all eschatological themes of the Bible, it also offers a key to the interpretation of Bible prophecy. That key is the future destiny of Israel.

But why Israel? The rabbis taught that God chose Israel because no other people would accept His revelation. The Midrash on Exodus (27:9) says, "When God was about to give the Torah, no other nation but Israel would accept it. . . . When God revealed himself on Sinai, there was not a nation at whose doors He did not knock, but they would not undertake to keep it; as soon as He came to Israel, they exclaimed: 'All that the Lord hath spoken will we do, and obey.' "

Does God see in the Jew something of greater merit than He saw in the Gentile? Something of such intrinsic value— like his mythical genius for religion—that, in spite of Israel's rejection of the Lord Jesus Christ, God is compelled to preserve them as a people? The rabbis believed that God did have a special love for Israel. In the Midrash they noticed that in Numbers 8:19 the words "the children of Israel" occur five times. So they said, "See how God loves the Israelites! In one single verse He names them five times! . . . So God yearns to make mention of Israel at every hour!"

Why should God still favor the Jew? This has been a source of consternation to many who study the prophetic Word. However, Ezekiel gives the answer:

> But I had regard for my holy name, which the house of Israel had profaned among the nations, whither they went. Therefore say unto the house of Israel, Thus saith the Lord Jehovah: I do not this for your sake, O house of Israel, but

for my holy name, which ye have profaned among the nations, whither ye went. And I will sanctify my great name, which hath been profaned among the nations, which ye have profaned in the midst of them; and the nations shall know that I am Jehovah, saith the Lord Jehovah, when I shall be sanctified in you before their eyes (36:21-23).

It is "not for your sake do I this, saith the Lord" (Eze 36:32). The Jew is to be regathered back to the land and he is to experience spiritual restoration (cf. vv. 25 ff.), but not because of any merit of his own. In fact, Israel has constantly failed the Lord and profaned His name, both while in the land before the exile and after she had been driven from the land (36:16-20). But in spite of this, the Lord must fulfill His promises to Israel because they were unconditionally made and thus His "holy name" (v. 22), His "great name" (v. 23), is at stake.

If God's promises to Israel, set forth in the covenant made with Abraham, were only conditionally made, then His vindication would not be necessary. He would have been faithful to His promises even if He had voided the covenant—the conditions not having been met by Israel. However, the terms of the Abrahamic covenant were made unconditionally.

God promised to bless Israel and to make her a spiritual blessing to all the nations. Though this promise did find fulfillment in the seed of Abraham which is the Lord Jesus Christ (Gal 3:16), it must yet find an extended fulfillment in the literal seed—the Jew. The name of God has been profaned by the Jew. Now it must be exalted by the Jew, for God must yet demonstrate in history that His original intentions for Israel are to be realized and that His program for the nation has not been frustrated by Israel's unfaithfulness. "Then the nations that are left round about you shall know that I, Jehovah, have builded the ruined places, and planted that which was desolate: I, Jehovah, have spoken it, and I will do it" (Eze 36:36).

But the literal fulfillment of the promises of God to Israel has been denied by some expositors on the basis of Jeremiah 18:7-10. Speaking in the light of the coming fall of Judah and the exile, Jeremiah said,

> At what instant I shall speak concerning a nation, and concerning a kingdom, to pluck up and to break down and to destroy it; if that nation, concerning which I have spoken, turn from their evil, I will repent of the evil that I thought to do unto them. And at what instant I shall speak concerning a nation, and concerning a kingdom, to build and to plant it; if they do that which is evil in my sight, that they obey not my voice, then I will repent of the good, wherewith I said I would benefit them.

Is there a principle here that must be applied to all of God's previous promises to Israel? Does this principle give all prophecy a conditional qualification? Though the covenant with Abraham was unconditionally given, must it now be understood only in the light of the conditional revision that the prophet Jeremiah seems to impose upon prophecy?

Even though it is insisted that the Abrahamic covenant was given unconditionally, and that the part of it which has been fulfilled has been fulfilled literally and therefore that which remains must also be literally fulfilled, we must also recognize that there are some *conditional principles of blessings that operate within the context of the unconditional ones.* Jeremiah is declaring that those promises which are conditionally made will be conditionally fulfilled, or they will be voided, depending upon the response of the nations involved. This simply recognizes that *some* of God's promises are conditional. However, it does not follow that *all* His promises are conditional. Even in this age of grace we have some unconditional and irrevocable promises to the believer—justification by faith, for example. But within this framework are conditional blessings that the believer might, or might not, receive, depending upon his obedience—answers to prayer, for example.

Thus the contingencies enunciated by Jeremiah do not necessarily reach up to void the unconditional nature of the covenant made with Abraham. It is in the light of this principle, which recognizes that there are conditional blessings offered within the context of the unconditional ones, that the prophet Hosea said that Israel could be both *Lo-ammi* ("not my people"), and *Ammi* ("my *people*") (Ho 1:9–2:1). By covenant they were the people of God, but by their actions they were not His people. The first is unconditional; the second is contingent.

Therefore, it is the unconditional and unalterable destiny of the nation Israel that gives direction to Bible prophecy. This is the main road down which we go, looking on either side for the correlatives which are the prophetic destinies of the church and the Gentile nations.

Israel plus the two correlatives of the church and the nations comprise the key to all Bible prophecy. This is also the key to the interpretation of Jesus' great prophetic discourse in Matthew 24–25.

God will bring Israel to her national destiny. The path of fulfillment will lead the nation through a long second exile in which she will know times of travail and of tribulation. After experiencing the horrors of the Roman invasion of the first century, she will be dispersed among the nations for two millenniums. As Hosea says, "For the children of Israel shall abide many days without king, and without prince, and without sacrifice, and without pillar, and without ephod or teraphim" (3:4). The suffering she endures will only preview the greater suffering that she is to endure in the latter days during the great-tribulation period. She will also be assaulted by false Messiahs, ranging from the trivial deceivers of the first century to the supreme impostor, the beast of the great tribulation.

But out of this experience of suffering and delusion and spiritual vacuum will come the glorious experience of recognizing the Lord Jesus Christ as the true Messiah of Israel when He returns to the earth a second time. Hosea says, "Afterward shall the children of Israel return, and seek Jehovah their God, and David their king, and shall come with fear unto Jehovah and to his goodness in the latter days" (3:5).

Involved in Israel's destiny will also be the destiny of the Gentile nations. For, said Jesus, the Jew "shall fall by the edge of the sword, and shall be led captive into all the nations: and Jerusalem shall be trodden down of the Gentiles, until the times of the Gentiles be fulfilled" (Lk 21:24). The long dominion of the Gentile nations over Israel will finally climax in the most profound and intense subjection that the nations have ever imposed upon the Jew. But for the elect's sake (i.e., Israel), this time will be shortened and the times of the Gentiles will come to a close with the great conflagration of Armageddon.

Those Gentile nations that have blessed Israel will in turn be blessed. Those that have cursed Israel will be cursed, according to the terms of the ancient covenant with Abraham. The five world empires, beginning with Babylon and terminating with the revived Roman Empire, will pass from the stage of history and the Lord Jesus Christ will "set up a kingdom which shall never be destroyed, nor shall the sovereignty thereof be left to another people; but it shall break in pieces and consume all these kingdoms, and it shall stand for ever" (Dan 2:44).

In the interim, between the first and second coming of Christ while God's prophetic time clock is stilled, the Lord is calling out a people for His name. They compose the church, the body of Christ. When the last believer that is to make up the body of Christ is added to the church through saving faith in the Lord Jesus, the trumpet will sound, the dead in Christ will arise, and all will be caught up together to meet the Lord in the air.

It is only after the church has been translated that the tribulation period will begin. The great parenthesis, which is the church age, closes with the rapture. At that point God's prophetic time clock for Israel begins to tick again. The pendulum which has hung unmoved for the last two thousand years while the mystery of the church was being formed, moves again to tick off the last seven years of God's temporal dealing with the nation Israel. It is then that the unfulfilled seventieth week of Daniel's great time prophecy will be completed (9:24 ff.).

And then Jesus will return in His glorious second coming. Israel, the church, and the blessed of the nations will enter the kingdom age. It is then that the beautiful picture of Amos 9:11-15 will be fulfilled:

> In that day will I raise up the tabernacle of David that is fallen, and close up the breaches thereof; and I will raise up its ruins, and I will build it as in the days of old; that they may possess the remnant of Edom, and all the nations that are called by my name, saith Jehovah that doeth this. Behold, the days come, saith Jehovah, that the plowman shall overtake the reaper, and the treader of grapes him that soweth seed; and the mountains shall drop sweet wine, and all the hills shall melt. And I will bring back the captivity of my people Israel, and they shall build the waste cities, and inhabit them; and they shall plant vineyards, and drink the wine thereof; they shall also make gardens, and eat the fruit of them. And I will plant them upon their land, and they shall no more be plucked up out of their land which I have given them, saith Jehovah thy God.

Subject Index

Alexander the Great, 93
Allegory of the foundling child, 25
Allenby, General, 78
Amillennial, 42, 147
Antichrist
  Antiochus Epiphanes, a type of, 94
  and apostate church, 88-90, 100-101
  covenants with Israel, 33, 74, 81, 101
  defeat of, 122
  defends Israel against Russia, 112
  end of reign of, 125
  as false god, 113-16
  during great tribulation, 100
  hostile toward saints, 87
  image of, in temple, 84, 114
  persecutes Jews, 101, 144
  and revived Roman Empire, 98
  rises to power, 91
  spiritual deceiver, 115-16
  as world dictator, 112-13
  worship of, by apostate church, 101
Antiochus IV Epiphanes, 94, 102-3, 106, 113-14, 116, 146
Anti-Semitism, 17
Arab-Israeli War of 1967, 18, 45, 84, 134
Ark of covenant, 80-81
Armageddon
  definition of, 119
  battle of, 118-22, 134, 140, 141
  ends times of gentiles, 44, 61, 122
  includes Orient, 121-22
  location of, 119-21
  time of, 121
Artaxerxes, 32
Asia, seven churches of, 63-68
Augustus, Caesar, 53, 114

Babylon, ecclesiastical, 88-90
Babylonian Empire, 93
Balfour Declaration, 77-78
Bar Kochba, 18, 45, 52-53, 82
Barnabas, epistle of, 82

China, Red, 134
Christ, judgment seat of, 71, 140, 144
Christs, false, 51-53

Church
  age of, 40, 63-68, 135-36
  apostate, in tribulation, 88-90, 136
  as body of Christ, 28, 43
  bounded by Pentecost and rapture, 43, 62
  created by baptism of Spirit, 29-30
  future of, 9-10, 13, 27
  in great parenthesis, 33, 152-53
  history of, on earth, 43-44
  and judgment of nations, 141
  mystery of, revealed, 22, 29
  not in tribulation, 67, 68, 69, 89
  not in view of O.T., 28
  not spiritual Israel, 43
  and Olivet Discourse, 132-39
  prophetic program for, 43-44
  as second interim mystery, 26-34
  to watch and occupy, 137
Cicero, 96
Claudius, 57
Common Market, European, 134
Constantine, 65, 66, 80, 82, 94
Covenants with Israel, 20
  Abrahamic, 21, 23, 43, 145, 149
  modified, 21
  broken by Antichrist, 101
  conditional, 20, 23, 150-51
  Davidic, 21, 23-24
  fulfilled literally, 22
  God will remember, 25, 125
  literal fulfillment of, denied, 149-50
  made by Antichrist, 33, 74
  New, 20, 21, 25
  Palestinian, 21, 22
  Sinai, 20, 21, 23
  still valid, 20
  unconditional, 20, 23, 150-51
Crowns, 71-72
Cult of the beast, 103
Cyrus the Great, 93

David, King, 18
  Bar Kochbah in line of, 53
  great Son of, 24
  line of, 53
  in line of Kings, 23-24
  tabernacle of, 25
Decision, valley of, 120

154

Scripture Index